# FAMOUS LIVES

## The Story of
# THURGOOD MARSHALL
### Justice for All

## By Joe Arthur

Gareth Stevens Publishing
**MILWAUKEE**

For a free color catalog describing Gareth Stevens' list of high-quality books and multimedia programs, call 1-800-542-2595 (USA) or 1-800-461-9120 (Canada). Gareth Stevens Publishing's Fax: (414) 225-0377.
See our catalog, too, on the World Wide Web: http://gsinc.com

Library of Congress Cataloging-in-Publication Data

Arthur, Joe.
   The story of Thurgood Marshall : justice for all / by Joe Arthur.
      p. c.m. – (Famous lives)
   Originally published: New York  : Bantam Doubleday Dell Books for Young Readers,
© 1995. (Dell yearling biography).
   Includes index.
   Summary: Presents the life of the first African-American appointed to the Supreme Court.
   ISBN 0-8368-1472-X (lib. bdg.)
   1. Marshall, Thurgood, 1908-1993–Juvenile literature. 2. United States. Supreme Court–
Biography–Juvenile literature. 3. Judges–United States–Biography–Juvenile literature.
   [1. Marshall, Thurgood, 1908-1993. 2. Judges. 3. United States. Supreme Court–Biography.
   4. African-Americans–Biography.] I. Title. II. Series: Famous lives (Milwaukee, Wis.)
   KF8745.M34A86  1996
   347.73'2634–dc20
   [B]                                                                 95-52872

The events described in this book are true. They have been carefully researched and excerpted from authentic biographies, writings, and commentaries. No part of this biography has been fictionalized. To learn more about Thurgood Marshall, refer to the list of books and videos at the back of this book or ask your librarian to recommend other fine books and videos.

First published in this edition in North America in 1996 by
**Gareth Stevens Publishing**
1555 North RiverCenter Drive, Suite 201
Milwaukee, Wisconsin 53212 USA

Original © 1995 by Parachute Press, Inc. as a Yearling Biography.
Published by arrangement with Bantam Doubleday Dell Books for Young Readers,
a division of Bantam Doubleday Dell Publishing Group, Inc.
Additional end matter © 1996 by Gareth Stevens, Inc.

The trademark Yearling® is registered in the U.S. Patent and Trademark Office.
The trademark Dell® is registered in the U.S. Patent and Trademark Office.

COVER PICTURE CREDIT: Harris and Ewing/Collection of the Supreme Court of the United States.

Printed in the United States of America

1 2 3 4 5 6 7 8 9 99 98 97 96

# Contents

# FAMOUS LIVES

*titles in Large-Print Editions:*

# Foreword

Once, when Thurgood Marshall was arguing a case before the Supreme Court, he was asked what he meant when he talked about people being equal. "Equal," Thurgood replied, "means getting the *same* thing, at the *same* time and in the *same* place." Thurgood Marshall liked being simple and to the point.

Thurgood Marshall was a lawyer. But he was not the average lawyer. He learned when he was very young that there were two sets of laws. One was for whites, the other for African-Americans like himself. While still a child in the early 1920s, Thurgood knew he faced racial *discrimination* every time he left his house. He knew that he might be taunted or rejected because of the color of his skin. He knew that if he was thirsty, he would not be allowed to order a soda at a drugstore soda fountain. He knew that he could even be beaten, and that the law would be on the side of his attacker.

And such practices were all *legal*. They were not against the law.

As he grew up, Thurgood Marshall made a decision to fight for full equality for *all* citizens.

Because of Thurgood Marshall, white and African-

1

American students no longer have to attend separate schools. And because he was this nation's first black Supreme Court justice, that Court has grown stronger. Thurgood Marshall helped open it to people of different backgrounds. Finally, because of Thurgood Marshall's life and work, the ideal of equal rights for all Americans is closer to reality.

# A Fighting Word

Fourteen-year-old Thurgood Marshall had a job to do. His boss wanted him to deliver four brand-new women's hats. That was easy enough. He'd done it many times since taking the after-school job at Schoen's Specialty Shop.

With the hatboxes in his arms, Thurgood stood on the street curb. He listened impatiently for the sound of the trolley. In 1922, trolley cars were the common way to get around in cities. Thurgood's straight-ahead vision was blocked by the hatboxes. But if he turned his head slowly, he could look to the side. What he saw there was the springtime sun glinting off the steel rails that ran down the middle of the street. Finally, a block away, the trolley came into view. Its bell clanged as it approached the intersection.

In another minute, Thurgood heard the conductor apply the brakes. When Thurgood judged the car to be nearly opposite him, he moved off the curb into the street. Groping his way, he stepped carefully up into the trolley's doorway.

Suddenly, Thurgood felt a hand grip his arm. Someone was pulling him backward.

Thurgood tried to keep his balance without dropping the boxes. Then he heard a man's voice behind him.

"Nigger," the man snarled, "don't you never push in front of no white lady again!"

The man had called him *nigger,* an ugly racial insult. Thurgood's father had told his son what to do if anyone ever called him that. "You got my permission to fight him," his father had instructed. "You got my *orders* to fight him!"

In a flash, Thurgood threw down the hatboxes. Spinning around, he found himself facing a middle-aged white man. A white woman stood next to the sneering man. Thurgood sprang forward. He swung his fist directly at the jaw of the man who had insulted him.

Years later Thurgood told a reporter, "I tore into him. I was beating this guy up pretty good."

Then the police arrived. The problem was, Thurgood lived in Baltimore, Maryland, only fifty-seven years after the *Civil War* had ended slavery. The war and slavery were over, but blacks and whites were not treated equally. In fact *Jim Crow laws* made it perfectly legal to keep blacks *segregated,* or separated, from whites.

Jim Crow laws were named after a song sung in nineteenth-century minstrel shows. A minstrel show was a comedy performance in which white actors painted their faces black. Jim Crow was a black character in the show, portrayed in an insulting way. Jim Crow laws prohibited African-Americans from eating in the same restaurants with whites. African-

4

Americans could not sit in the same part of a movie theater or attend the same school as whites. And under no circumstances could a black person hit a white person.

Thurgood was aware of segregation every time he rode the streetcar. That day was no different. He knew the rules: African-Americans were expected to step aside at trolley stops and let the whites get on the car first. Then African-Americans were expected to ride in the back of the car. Thurgood knew that black men had been dragged from their homes and lynched—usually by being hanged by their necks until dead—for doing less than what he had just done. Only three years before, he'd been shocked to read in the newspaper about a black man named Bragg Williams who was taken from his Texas jail cell by a mob and killed. And the state police hadn't raised a finger to stop it.

Thurgood had never seen anything like a lynching in person, but he had already had his fill of segregation. There was one incident he'd never forget. It was the kind of experience a student would write about if the teacher assigned an essay called "The most embarrassing thing that ever happened to you." It was a Saturday and Thurgood was shopping in Baltimore's business district. He had to go to the bathroom, but there weren't any rest rooms for "Colored Only." The stores that gladly took their African-American customers' money refused to provide them with rest rooms. Hurrying, Thurgood caught the trolley home, then raced up the sidewalk to his front door. He didn't make it in time. Thurgood Marshall never forgave the discrimination that made such an "accident" happen.

Now, standing in the middle of the street next to the trolley, Thurgood knew he was in big trouble. Would the police even listen to his side of the story?

Army Matthews was the police officer on duty. He was a white man assigned to a mostly black neighborhood. Matthews was known and respected by the community. As a sergeant, he had commanded African-American soldiers during World War I. He had learned to judge men by their deeds, not the color of their skin.

After separating Thurgood and the white man, Officer Matthews asked them what started the fight. The white man immediately began shouting that Thurgood attacked him for no reason.

Thurgood was so upset that he had to pause to catch his breath. Then, as calmly as he could, he explained what the white man had called him. He also told Officer Matthews that he hadn't seen the white woman, or the white man either, for that matter. He was only going about his job of delivering hats for Schoen's Specialty Shop. He pointed out that Mr. Schoen designed hats for some of the finest ladies in Baltimore. Even Mrs. Woodrow Wilson, the wife of the former president, fancied Mr. Schoen's designs.

Thurgood went on to explain that the hats were nearly worth their weight in gold. Mr. Schoen got as much as $150 for one of his creations. Now those valuable hats were lying in the street.

"I saw it all," a tall, elderly African-American man

told Officer Matthews. Looking around, Thurgood recognized Mr. Truesdale, a friend of his father's. Mr. Truesdale confirmed Thurgood's story.

A small crowd had gathered. Everyone watched closely, waiting to see what would happen next. The white man did not deny calling Thurgood a nigger. And Thurgood did not deny hitting him.

Officer Matthews hesitated, but finally made his decision. He had to do his duty. He cleared his throat and spoke firmly. "You're under arrest," he said to Thurgood Marshall.

# A Family Heritage
## of Protest

At the police station, Thurgood was formally charged with hitting the white man. Army Matthews, the arresting officer, led Thurgood to a telephone where he could make one call.

Thurgood called Mortimer Schoen, his boss and the owner of the expensive hats that he had thrown to the pavement.

Mr. Schoen told Thurgood he had witnessed the fight—and had heard what the white man called Thurgood. Mr. Schoen did not approve of such language. He told his young employee that he would come right down to the police station and help him.

Mr. Schoen paid the fifty-dollar fine to get Thurgood released. And he never said a word about the young man having to pay him back.

"I'm really sorry that I busted up your hats in that fight," Thurgood told his boss.

"Was it worth it?" Mr. Schoen asked him.

Thurgood hesitated a moment. Remembering what the white man called him, he said, "It sure was."

Years later Thurgood told a reporter he had learned some important lessons from that experience.

First, he said, he learned that there are good people as well as bad in all races. He compared the actions of Mr. Schoen to the behavior of the white man at the trolley stop. And Thurgood also realized that life for a black person in the South was dangerous. He would have to be careful.

When Thurgood was safe at home, he told his parents about what had happened. The last thing they wanted was for one of their sons to go to jail. At the same time, both parents were proud that Thurgood stood up to the racial insult.

Actually, Thurgood wasn't the first person in his family to stand up to racial discrimination. He loved to hear his parents talk proudly about their African roots. What he heard were tales of independent, strong-willed men and women.

No one in the family knew the name of Thurgood's great-grandfather on his father's side. But his reputation was a family legend. Thurgood's great-grandfather was a slave. But the story is that he was such a problem to his owner, the owner finally got fed up and set him free. When the disgusted slave owner released Thurgood's great-grandfather, he told the newly freed slave, "I'm going to set you free—on one condition. Get . . . out of this county and never come back."

Thurgood's great-grandfather left, but he didn't go too far. He settled just a few miles down the road. He got married, acquired a farm, and stayed right there, close to his old master, but now proudly free, for the rest of his life.

Thurgood's grandfather was called Thorough

9

Good Marshall. He had fought for the *Union,* or Northern side, in the Civil War. Before he joined the army, Grandfather Marshall had always been called simply Marshall. When he joined the Union Army, he was told he needed a first and middle name. He thought about it a moment, then picked Thorough Good out of thin air.

Thurgood was named after his grandfather Marshall. His legal name was Thoroughgood. But when he started school, Thoroughgood worried that the other kids might make fun of his name. They might call him "Thorough Goodie Two-Shoes." He certainly didn't want that. Besides, when he was learning to write, he found the name just took too long to put down on paper. In the second grade, without asking anyone about it, Thoroughgood Marshall shortened his name to Thurgood.

Thurgood's grandmother on his father's side was Annie Marshall. She was famous in the family for her sit-down strike. A sit-down strike occurs when someone sits down and refuses to move, keeping people from doing their work. Annie conducted her strike around the turn of the century, when Baltimore was being wired for electricity. Without much notice, the Baltimore Gas and Electric Company told Annie that they were going to erect a street light right in front of her grocery store. Annie told them, no, they weren't, not even if they were to ask her properly. Besides, the pole would spoil her view of the street.

The power company went to court and won. They were permitted to erect the pole. But when the company spokesman told Annie of the judge's ruling, it didn't change her mind one bit. When the electric company truck showed up to place the pole, the men found Annie's rocking chair parked right in the middle of the spot where the pole was supposed to go. And Annie was sitting in the chair! She refused to move. She sat there all day for three days until the electric company finally gave up.

There were fighters and independent thinkers on Thurgood's mother's side of the family, too. His mother's father, Isaiah Olive Branch Williams, had made his living as a sailor. When he decided to settle down, he chose to live in Baltimore. He had visited that port city many times as a sailor.

Isaiah saw that African-Americans were not well treated in Baltimore. He called a meeting in the black community on August 5, 1875, to demand that the police stop beating the city's black residents. At that time, the *Ku Klux Klan* was trying to gain control of Maryland state politics. The Ku Klux Klan, founded in 1869 in Tennessee, had an all-white membership that hid their identities behind white sheets and hoods. Blacks hated the Ku Klux Klan. Klansmen terrorized and killed Southern blacks who tried to vote or to exercise any of their other rights as American citizens. The black community was proud, but also a little nervous, when Isaiah stood up to protest. The beatings stopped for a while, but it would take more than one protest meeting to stop the violent attacks against African-Americans.

After Isaiah settled in Baltimore, he married and began to raise a family. Because he had always loved literature and the opera, he and his wife, Mary Eliza,

11

named their children after fictional characters or places he admired. A son was given the name Avon, after William Shakespeare's hometown in England. A daughter was named Delicia. Delicia is a character in one of Shakespeare's plays. And another daughter was called Norma Arica. Years before, Isaiah had been in Arica, Chile. While he was there, he had seen *Norma,* an opera written by Vincenzo Bellini. The opera and the city were combined to create the girl's name. After Norma Arica grew up and got married, it was she who became Thurgood's mother.

Norma Williams and William Marshall, Thurgood's father, had known each other in their neighborhood and in school. Both their parents ran grocery stores. Norma's interest in music and the theater was as strong as her father's, but she knew she had to be practical. She had to make a living. Norma graduated from Coppin Normal College, an all-black school, and took a job as an elementary school teacher.

William held many jobs during his life. At one time he was a Pullman car porter for the B&O (Baltimore & Ohio) Railroad. Pullman cars offered overnight train passengers a tiny sleeping space. As a porter, Mr. Marshall carried luggage for the passengers, made up their beds, and called out the stops as the train made its run.

Once, William Marshall walked off a job because a boss made a rude comment about African-Americans. William had strong opinions about how black and whites got along, and he would not tolerate disrespect.

William and Norma got married in 1904. He was

twenty-one and she was seventeen. Aubrey, the Marshalls' first son, arrived that same year. Four years later, on July 2, 1908, Thurgood Marshall was born.

Norma wanted very much for her children to grow up to be successful. She told her sons over and over again how important education is. She said whatever they wanted in life, they would have to work hard to earn. Like most parents, William and Norma wanted their children to do better than they had done. Because there were so few black doctors serving black neighborhoods, Norma told Aubrey he should study medicine when he grew up. She wanted Thurgood to become a dentist.

Thurgood's mother was forceful and direct in raising her sons. When she wanted them to do something, she told them in plain and simple language. Thurgood's father, on the other hand, preferred to guide his sons by example. To spend more time with his family, the elder Marshall gave up working on the railroad. That job kept him away from home too much. Instead, he took a job as a chief steward at the Gibson Island Country Club. Located on Maryland's Chesapeake Bay, the club had a wealthy, all-white membership. Every day when William went to work, he had to go in through the servants' entrance.

Although William Marshall was glad to be home at night with his family, he missed the railroad. He loved trains. He was fascinated with the powerful steam locomotives, how they looked, and how they sounded. Even if he didn't work on the railroad anymore, he could still see trains at the station. When his sons were young, he enjoyed taking them down to the B&O

13

depot just to watch the passenger trains come and go. Thurgood discovered he shared his father's interest in trains. As a result, railroads became something of a hobby for him. When Thurgood was a grown man, one holiday season his co-workers bought him an electric train set. He liked it so much he kept it set up in his apartment. Wearing an engineer's cap, he relaxed after work by running his railroad. There, he liked to point out, he was the boss.

William Marshall influenced Thurgood in another, more important way. William loved to argue. He would debate anyone who cared to discuss politics. He was particularly interested in law and justice. In his spare time, Thurgood's father went down to the courthouse and sat in on whatever trial was being held. He would listen to the lawyers and think about how he would decide the case. Then he'd tell his family about what he'd seen. Aubrey and Thurgood were always pulled into his discussions. Aubrey wasn't much for arguing, but Thurgood took after his father.

Years later, Thurgood told a news reporter that his father "never told me to become a lawyer, but he turned me into one. . . . He taught me how to argue, [and he] challenged my logic on every point, by making me prove every statement I made, even if I were discussing the weather."

# Banished to the Basement

T hurgood Marshall was a good baby. In fact, his nickname was "Goody." That may have been short for Thoroughgood. But he may partly have gotten the name because he was very timid. By the time Thurgood was five years old, he had changed. He became tough and less easy to handle. His family had moved to New York City not long after Thurgood was born. An aunt thought that perhaps the new neighborhood had changed Thurgood. In New York, the family lived in a cramped apartment at 140th Street and Lenox Avenue, in Harlem. And New York City was a lot tougher than Baltimore. In New York City, a boy had to be tough.

Thurgood's family lived in New York City for five years. One of the reasons they had gone there was to allow Mrs. Marshall to improve her education. She attended classes at Columbia University's Teachers College. But by 1914, when Thurgood was six years old, the family was ready to return to Baltimore.

Back in their hometown, the Marshalls moved into a row house. Years later Thurgood told an interviewer that the alley behind their house marked the

15

dividing line between the safe neighborhood and the rough one. "We lived on a respectable street," he recalled, "but behind us there were back alleys where the roughnecks and the tough kids hung out." Thurgood's older brother, Aubrey, always stayed in the front yard to play. Thurgood, on the other hand, liked to play in the alley with the tough kids. "When it was time for dinner," he once remarked, "my mother used to go to the front door and call my older brother. Then she'd go to the *back* door and call me."

Thurgood got along with his older brother most of the time. But Aubrey didn't always approve of Thurgood's behavior. He thought Thurgood caused their mother too many problems. Thurgood was ten when Aubrey decided to deal with Thurgood in a language his younger brother could understand. He beat him up. It happened when their mother sent the boys to the market to buy food for dinner. Purchases made, the two boys piled the grocery sacks on their wagon. While they were pulling it home, the wagon tipped over. The groceries spilled out all over the street. Thurgood immediately blamed Aubrey. "You big dummy!" he yelled. Then, for good measure, he added, "You clumsy fool!"

Aubrey slugged his brother—but the fight didn't last very long. Thurgood wasn't strong enough to beat thirteen-year-old Aubrey. The two boys never fought again.

Mrs. Marshall taught at the same elementary school that Thurgood attended. This was a fine arrangement from her point of view. She could keep an eye on her active son. And Thurgood didn't mind, either.

He figured that the principal and the other teachers wouldn't punish him too harshly if he got out of line. They wouldn't want to face his mother. Thurgood had it figured right. He got away with a lot. He was often late with his homework. He didn't study enough for quizzes. And he enjoyed being the class clown.

All through school, Thurgood had part-time jobs. He got his first job when he was seven. He was a delivery boy for Hale's Grocery, a store in his neighborhood. And after working as a hat delivery boy for Schoen's Specialty Shop, Thurgood was hired as a waiter on the B&O Railroad. He worked on the train's run between New York City and Washington, D.C. He also spent one summer working at the Gibson Island Country Club to earn money for college.

Thurgood Marshall attended Baltimore's Frederick Douglass High School. The high school was named after the former slave who spoke out against slavery long before the Civil War began. Frederick Douglass may have fought for equal rights, but black students in the school named after him did not have equal rights. Frederick Douglass High School was, by law, a black high school. Across town was another high school. It was for white students only. The two schools had nothing to do with each other. Athletic teams were segregated and did not play against one another. And the schools held separate dances. Blacks and whites may have lived in the same city, even on the same streets sometimes, but when it came to the public schools, they were totally separate.

When he entered high school, young Thurgood was not particularly concerned with matters of racial equality. Nor was he as devoted a student as his brother. Aubrey had gone to Frederick Douglass before Thurgood, and was an excellent student. Thurgood just got by. His grades were decent enough, but he put little effort into his subjects. The only book Thurgood admitted studying diligently was the football team's playbook. He enjoyed playing on the school's team. And he was a social person, spending his time with friends. Thurgood even led a small group of teenagers. It was mostly boys, but there were three girls in it as well. The group played pranks on fellow students and occasionally cut classes.

Thurgood was very popular with the girls. He said he never lacked for a date in high school, and claimed to have been a better-than-average dancer. This was during the 1920s, when young people were listening to jazz and doing fast dances like the Charleston.

Thurgood's principal at Frederick Douglass was Mr. Lee. Mr. Lee was worried about Thurgood. He thought the boy could grow up to be successful, but he wasn't serious enough. Trying to help Thurgood, Mr. Lee gave him detention. He made Thurgood stay in the dreary school basement. The first time, Mr. Lee pointed Thurgood to a chair and handed him a copy of the United States *Constitution*. Each time Thurgood was in detention, he was told to sit on that chair and study a particular article, section, or amendment. The first time this happened, Thurgood wanted to know how long he would have to stay in the basement. Mr. Lee told him he'd have to stay until he knew the passage by heart.

Thurgood did as he was told. He repeated each

section over and over to himself. Then he'd go to Mr. Lee's office and recite the memorized part.

Thurgood was sent to the basement so often that he wound up memorizing the entire Constitution. But he didn't only learn the words. In the many hours he spent in that dank basement, he learned their meaning, too. Thurgood was especially interested in the Thirteenth, Fourteenth, and Fifteenth amendments.

The Thirteenth Amendment was passed in 1865, right after the end of the Civil War. It outlawed slavery in the United States. The Fourteenth, added to the Constitution in 1868, guaranteed equal rights to former slaves. Two years later, the states ratified the Fifteenth Amendment. It gave black men the right to vote.

Some of the language in the Constitution is hard to understand. When Thurgood wasn't sure what some of the words meant, he'd repeat them at home for his father. It was at the age of thirteen that Thurgood asked his father a tough question. If the Constitution guarantees equal rights for all Americans, Thurgood wanted to know, why didn't black citizens have those rights?

William Marshall answered his son by saying that the Constitution is only a blueprint. It is a guide telling the American people how things should be. It does not describe the way they actually are. He told Thurgood that it's up to each person to help make the promises of the Constitution come true. When that happened, he continued, the United States would have a system that is fair to all people.

William Marshall was never too busy to answer

19

Thurgood's questions. He loved to discuss issues with his sons, especially issues about the law. And both Mr. and Mrs. Marshall always taught their children that what they thought was as important as what they did.

Studying the Constitution raised serious questions in Thurgood's mind about law and equality. So did the police station next door to Frederick Douglass High School. In those days, before air conditioning, everybody opened their windows when the weather turned warm and humid. At such times, Thurgood and the other students could hear the cries of black prisoners who were being beaten by the Baltimore police during questioning. Thurgood never forgot those cries.

Thurgood was sixteen when he was graduated from high school. The year was 1925. There was no question of what lay ahead for Thurgood. From the time her children were old enough to walk, Norma Marshall had told her sons they were going to college. Aubrey had gone away to Lincoln University, a private black college in Pennsylvania.

The University of Maryland would have been Thurgood's first choice. The school had a good academic reputation and was close to home. Unfortunately, the University of Maryland did not admit blacks.

Thurgood decided on Lincoln. Whenever Aubrey came home for the holidays or vacation, Thurgood listened to his brother's tales of campus life at the school. The more Thurgood heard, the better the school sounded. He knew that he could get an excellent education at Lincoln. In the fall, Thurgood joined his brother at the Chester, Pennsylvania, college.

20

# Balcony Seating Only

Thurgood Marshall turned seventeen the July before he went away to Lincoln University. But for a while that summer, it looked as though he might not be able to go to college at all. He'd been accepted by the school's admissions office, but he didn't have a scholarship. This meant he had to pay his own tuition. It came to more than $300 a year—a lot of money in 1925. Thurgood worked all summer for the B&O Railroad and he saved what he earned. But as September neared, he didn't have enough money.

Norma Marshall knew how important a college education was. "You're going," she told Thurgood firmly. As a last resort, she headed downtown to a pawn shop. Removing both her wedding and engagement rings, she borrowed enough money on the jewelry to cover the rest of Thurgood's tuition.

Lincoln University was a highly respected, all-black college. Many of its professors were graduates of outstanding Ivy League schools such as Princeton, Yale, and Harvard. Because of Lincoln's high standards, many of its graduates had gone on to make names for themselves in their professions and in higher education. While Thurgood was a student at Lincoln, the poet Langston Hughes also attended classes there. He

21

and Thurgood became close friends. Cab Calloway also attended Lincoln. Calloway's jazz band was very popular and sold many records during the 1930s.

As a college student, Thurgood was a stylish and handsome young man. He wore his hair straight, combed back on the top and sides. Such a slick look was very popular at the time. He had heavy-lidded brown eyes that were large and appealing. And behind his tall, muscular frame and good looks was a casual, friendly student. He was also taking full advantage of being away from home for the first time in his life.

And what a time it was. Historians call that era the Roaring Twenties. America's young people had greater freedom then than at any time before. To add to his sense of freedom, Thurgood discovered he didn't have to work very hard at studying. Just as in high school, he could get average grades in college without studying very hard. And by then, he did not want to be a dentist. He had enrolled in pre-dentistry classes only to please his mother. He didn't want to disappoint her dream for him. But now, there were other things—fun things—he would rather be doing. He was, for instance, one of the founding members of Lincoln University's Weekend Club. It was called the Weekend Club because the sole purpose was to spend Friday night through Sunday having fun. Thurgood liked to boast about how little studying he did on weekends, while still managing to keep up passing grades. To help pay for his active social life, Thurgood learned how to play cards for money.

There are those who recall that Thurgood, like many other college students of that time, enjoyed drinking alcohol. Alcohol was illegal during the 1920s. Called Prohibition, the Eighteenth Amendment had been added to the Constitution. It outlawed the manufacture, transportation, and sale of alcohol. But it was a law often ignored by people—including college students. Lincoln students held their noisiest and liveliest parties on Saturday nights after football games. The celebrating was all the wilder when the team won, although that wasn't too often. The school happened to have a pretty bad team at the time Thurgood was a student.

One time Thurgood was called before the dean. He was accused of hazing freshmen. Hazing is the practice of teasing or harassing younger students. The upperclassmen would ridicule the young men or try to make them do foolish things. Sometimes the freshmen were ordered to do hundreds of push-ups, or to swallow live goldfish. Swallowing goldfish was a popular prank at the time. What Thurgood and some of his friends did was shave the heads of several freshmen. But Lincoln had rules against hazing. Such pranks were degrading and could be dangerous to the victim. Thurgood could have been expelled because of the incident. Instead, the hearing officer decided to suspend him for two weeks. The punishment hurt, but it didn't stop Thurgood's adventurous ways. He next became involved in a strike demanding better food in the dormitory cafeteria. The food issue, however, wasn't the only reason for the strike. Many Lincoln students, including Thurgood, believed that the all-white faculty didn't care enough about the students' welfare.

Because Lincoln University is in the North, many

black students made an assumption about the school. They thought it would be free of the racial segregation found in the South. But they discovered this was not the case. Thurgood and his fellow students learned early on that there was a big gap between the law and what was actually happening. Pennsylvania did have laws stating that public places were open to all races. But blacks and whites were still kept apart by tradition. Anti-segregation laws were never enforced.

One college experience, Thurgood said later, helped him make up his mind to spend his life fighting for *civil rights*. The incident came about because of Thurgood's love of Western movies.

There was only one theater in the area, in the nearby small town of Oxford. It wasn't hard to keep track of what movie was playing there. Thurgood recalled really wanting to see a certain cowboy film. When his friend Cranston Harewood asked him and five other Lincoln buddies to go, Thurgood eagerly said yes. They drove over to Oxford in Cranston's Model T Ford.

Thurgood and his friends had been to this theater before. They knew that the seating was segregated. African-Americans were required to sit high up in the balcony, separate from white people. On this particular evening, it wasn't Thurgood's idea to challenge the theater's seating rule. One of the other students, a man named U. S. Tate, made the suggestion. "He was the leader who said we ought to do something about it," Thurgood remembered years later.

Just as they always had done, Thurgood and his friends bought their tickets from the young woman in the box office. Then, the seven of them walked boldly past the stairs leading to the "Colored" balcony. Entering the main floor, the area for whites only, they found seats and settled in to watch the movie.

A white man sitting behind the students spoke up. "Niggers," he said, "why don't you just get out of here and sit where you belong?"

The seven students stayed right where they were. Even when they heard footsteps coming down the aisle toward them, the young men kept their seats.

An usher stopped at their row. He told them they were supposed to be sitting in the balcony and ordered them to move up there. Thurgood told the usher no, they weren't moving. They'd paid their money and they were going to sit where they wanted to.

The usher hesitated, then walked back to the lobby. Thurgood and the others were shaking from fear of what might happen next. But nothing did. They sat through the movie, and to their surprise, the white man behind them said nothing more. The manager, too, left them alone.

When it came time to leave the theater, the students were fearful that something might yet happen. Maybe there would be a mob of angry whites outside. Or maybe someone would vandalize Cranston's car.

The friends stuck very close together on their way out. They were relieved to see the lobby was empty. They were even more relieved when they found the street deserted and the old Ford right where they'd parked it.

They had desegregated the theater and nothing had happened!

From that night on, skin color never again determined where a moviegoer could sit in the Oxford theater. The incident was Thurgood Marshall's first attempt at helping desegregate one small corner of America, and it was a success.

In his sophomore year, Thurgood joined the college debating club. His booming baritone voice and forceful delivery earned him the nickname "Wrathful Marshall." The team defeated some well-known white colleges, in no small part because of Wrathful's speaking skills. Thurgood recalled fondly the many discussions with his father at the dining room table back home. He wrote his parents, "If I were taking debate for credit, I would be the biggest honor student they ever had around here."

Thurgood had developed a healthy respect for the power of the spoken word, especially when it is spoken with emotion. At a football pep rally the night before the homecoming game in 1929, Thurgood gave a fired-up speech. The team was having its usual terrible record that year. But with powerful words and emotion, Thurgood urged the players on to victory. After Thurgood's inspiring words, the team fought to a scoreless tie. The student body considered the contest a moral victory. Naturally, Thurgood took at least some of the credit.

Thurgood went out with a lot of young women while he was in college. Along with his party buddies, Thurgood attended the Cherry Street Memorial Church in Philadelphia because they had learned that was where many young women went. He later claimed to have been engaged "at *least* nine times," before he decided to get married.

Vivian Burey was the young woman who finally won Thurgood's heart. Nicknamed Buster, she was a student at the University of Pennsylvania and a year ahead of Thurgood. Once he met Buster, Thurgood stopped dating his other girlfriends. The young couple saw each other mostly on weekends. Sometimes they went to the movies in Oxford. Buster was greatly impressed when Thurgood told her of his part in desegregating the theater. Buster sensed that Thurgood Marshall might not be just another college man.

Thurgood and Buster fell in love. "First we decided to get married five years after I graduated," Thurgood recalled, "then three, then one."

Buster's parents did not approve. Buster and Thurgood were only twenty. They were not even legally adults. Buster, however, was firm about wanting to marry Thurgood.

Thurgood's parents liked Buster. But they, too, were against the couple getting married so young. Thurgood heard the same arguments from his parents that Buster heard from hers. In addition, Thurgood's mother feared the added responsibility of a wife and home might cause Thurgood to drop out of school.

In spite of all the advice from their parents, Thurgood and Buster went ahead with the marriage anyway. The wedding took place on September 4, 1929. The young couple found a small apartment in Oxford, not far from the movie theater, and settled down to married life. It was Thurgood's senior year.

Buster was a very good influence on Thurgood. She calmed him down. Although she herself was fun-loving and adventurous, she knew when to stop. And she knew when to tell Thurgood he should stop, too. Thurgood took his wife's good advice. He went to fewer parties and spent more nights at home studying. In fact, his study habits improved so much that he would graduate with honors later that year.

Buster had graduated from college the year before. She went to work to help meet expenses. After work, she cooked and cleaned the couple's small apartment, making it a comfortable home. But most important of all, Buster kept reminding her husband that he was destined for something great. She told him he could make a difference.

Thurgood agreed with Buster. What he wasn't sure about was the field of work he should choose. Thurgood thought about his future all through his last year in college. He had not done well in his pre-dentistry classes, and didn't want to be a dentist anyway.

When he broke the news to his mother, he was glad that she didn't seem too disappointed. After all, it had been her great dream that he become a dentist. Still, Thurgood had to make a living at something. He just didn't know what.

Thurgood Marshall's childhood experiences played a part in his decision about what to do for a living. There were those hours he spent reading the Constitution in the school basement. And there were the times his father talked about cases and lawyers he'd watched downtown at the courthouse. In college, Thurgood Marshall had learned that he had the ability to sway people with his dramatic voice and the force of a good argument. All of these lessons, all of his life's experiences, pointed him in the direction of law. Thurgood told Buster and then his family what he'd been thinking. He wanted to become a lawyer.

In 1930, Thurgood applied for admission to the University of Maryland Law School. Located in College Park, the school was only a short trolley ride from his parents' home. Thurgood had already decided that he wanted to practice law in Baltimore. The University of Maryland would give him a solid background in Maryland state law. He could then offer himself to the public as a hometown lawyer with a hometown law degree.

Perhaps Thurgood remembered how easily he and his friends had integrated the Oxford movie theater. Even though Thurgood wouldn't have been accepted at the University of Maryland four years ago because he was black, now he was applying to the university's law school. This might prove a different experience. Whatever Thurgood's thinking might have been, he applied to the law school with the deep hope of being admitted.

When a letter arrived from the law school, Thurgood eagerly tore open the envelope. The message, after all, held the key to his future. Scanning the letter hurriedly, Thurgood saw it was from an aide to the university president, R. A. Pearson. The university, Thurgood read, was turning him down. But, the letter went on to explain, the state of Maryland had

29

an offer. It would pay the difference between what it would have cost Thurgood to attend the University of Maryland and the tuition of school somewhere else, a school that "accepts Negroes." Thurgood Marshall was being denied admission to the law school because of his race.

A wave of anger surged over the young, would-be lawyer. It had been the same story all his life. By state and local laws, he had been required to attend all-black schools. Someday, Thurgood knew, this would have to be changed.

# "Freebie Lawyer"

Thurgood and Buster talked over his rejection by the Maryland law school. One part of him wanted to take a stand against segregation. He remembered clearly what he and his friends had done at the Oxford theater. But another voice in Thurgood's mind was telling him to complete his education first. There would be plenty of time later to seek justice. Furthermore, the country at the time was in the midst of the Great *Depression*. Thousands of men and women were out of work. Many were struggling just to put food on their tables. Thurgood sensed that the time to take a stand wasn't right yet. But one day it would be. One day he would challenge segregation at the university. In the meantime, he would find another law school, one that "accepts Negroes."

Thurgood Marshall chose Howard University in Washington, D.C. When he sent in his application, the university was called "the premier colored school" in the nation. Opened two years after the Civil War ended, Howard had produced many of America's black doctors, scientists, architects, and educators.

Howard's law school opened in 1869. It held classes

only at night until 1924, when Charles Hamilton Houston arrived. Houston was an African-American lawyer, well known in his field. He had graduated with honors from Amherst College and earned his law degree at Harvard Law School. Hired as a lecturer at Howard, Houston had been promoted to dean by the time Thurgood enrolled. Houston tirelessly dedicated himself to building a first-class law school for blacks. He oversaw the establishment of a full-time program. It was also his dream to turn out highly skilled lawyers who could attack Jim Crow laws, the laws that allowed blacks and whites to be separated in public places.

Thurgood and Buster moved to Baltimore from their apartment in Oxford. William and Norma Marshall gave a special graduation present to their son and daughter-in-law. They allowed the young couple to set up their new home on the third floor of the Marshall's Baltimore house.

Living with Thurgood's parents would cut down on expenses during law school. Thurgood did not have a scholarship for his studies. And there was no financial aid or student loans available during the depression years of the 1930s.

The same summer he was applying to Howard, Thurgood took a job at the country club where his father was employed as head steward. He needed the job badly to pay his tuition. Thurgood was assigned to wait on tables in the club dining room. It was not always pleasant work. The men and women who were members of the club were very rich and looked down on the African-Americans who worked there.

One night, a U.S. senator said to Thurgood, "Nigger, I want service at this table!"

Thurgood was angry, but he didn't say anything. He just smiled and took the politician's order.

Thurgood's father overheard what the senator had said, and he was furious—at the senator and at Thurgood.

"Thurgood," he told his son sharply, "you are a disgrace to the colored people!"

Thurgood admitted that the senator had called him by that hated name before. Several times, in fact. Mr. Marshall demanded to know how Thurgood could put up with such behavior.

Thurgood explained calmly. The name did hurt, but the senator always left a twenty dollar tip. "In a few days," Thurgood told his father, "I got myself almost enough money to pay off all my bills."

Clearly, Thurgood's days as a carefree student were behind him. When fall came, he started classes at Howard. He found law school to be very difficult. The train ride alone into Washington, D.C., was forty miles. Thurgood had to get up at five-thirty each morning to catch the train. He attended classes until three, then he went to work to help pay his expenses.

One way law schools train lawyers is to hold mock, or pretend, trials. Mock trials are conducted just like real ones. Law students and sometimes the instructors play all the different parts. In the many mock trials held in his classes, Thurgood soon earned a reputation as a skilled courtroom lawyer. He discovered he could out-argue all of the other students in his class. Thurgood knew he was successful only because of hard work. Before a mock trial began, he spent long hours preparing his case. Thurgood found that he especially enjoyed library research. He enjoyed tracking down *precedents,* past court decisions in similar cases.

While Thurgood was arguing a case in law school one time, a classmate noticed that Thurgood held his head high and slightly back. The young man commented that this reminded him of a turkey. Thurgood got as big a laugh out of the comment as the rest of the group. He also picked up a life-long nickname. From then on, his close friends called him Turkey.

Charles Houston often sat in on the mock trials. Thurgood got to know him well and came to admire him greatly. "Charles Houston was one of the greatest lawyers I've ever been privileged to know," Thurgood once told a reporter. "He was a perfectionist of the first order. . . . He banged our heads with his belief in dedication."

Dean Houston recognized Thurgood's abilities. This did not mean that Thurgood was the teacher's pet. But the young law student felt honored to be getting the attention of a man he so respected. If anything, Houston's approval drove Thurgood to excel all the more.

Thurgood graduated magna cum laude, with great distinction, in 1933. He was first in his class. Harvard University offered the young lawyer a fellowship. A fellowship is a type of scholarship that allows a graduate to continue his or her studies, or to do research, all expenses paid. It was a once-in-a-lifetime chance. Not many people got such opportunities, especially during a depression, when jobs and money were scarce. And not only was the fellowship an impressive honor. It also meant that Thurgood and Buster would have a steady income. Thurgood knew there were a lot of sensible reasons for accepting the fellowship.

But Thurgood turned it down. He had other plans. He had suffered too many slights over the years because of his race. He had been discriminated against too many times. When it came to the treatment of African-Americans, he believed the Constitution was being ignored. If he could make some small contribution toward ending discrimination and segregation, that was what he most wanted to do. And he wanted to do it right in his own home state.

With this goal in mind, Thurgood went into private practice. He rented space on the sixth floor of the Phoenix Building on the edge of downtown Baltimore. It would be a law office open to all people, however poor they might be.

With Buster at his side, Thurgood shopped for second-hand furniture. His mother gave him the Persian rug that her father had brought back from one of his voyages many years before. The beautiful antique rug was put down on Thurgood's office floor.

Starting out as a young lawyer was a struggle. When he could pay his secretary, a woman he called Little Bits, her salary was $7.50 a week. "Sometimes we'd be the only two people in that office for weeks at a time," Thurgood once told an interviewer.

"The phone company would call up," Thurgood added, "and say that they were going to disconnect my phone. I would bluff and say, 'You gonna discon-

35

nect *my* phone? Do you realize I'm a lawyer? You mess with my phone and I'll sue you until *you* pay *me*. . . . ' And they'd say, 'It's all right, Mr. Marshall, it's all right.' "

The fact was, there were many people in Baltimore who would have gladly hired Thurgood. They just couldn't afford it. In the deep South—places like Mississippi and Alabama—there had long been a tradition regarding African-Americans who needed legal services. They would go to see the local white judge, who would listen to their problem. Then, if whites in the area thought the person to be a "good Negro," the judge would give that person free legal advice. When African-Americans moved out of the deep South, it was a shock to many of them when they learned that things weren't the same "way up South" in places like Baltimore. One day an old woman, a recent migrant from the deep South, came into Thurgood's law office. She told him she had a legal matter to discuss with him. She'd gone to another lawyer, but he wanted money. The problem was she didn't have any. But the other lawyer did suggest she talk to Mr. Marshall. "He said you're a freebie lawyer," she told Thurgood. He chuckled, then took her case—free of charge.

Buster understood that Thurgood's law practice was growing very slowly. She scrimped to make ends meet. The first year Thurgood was in legal practice, he lost between three thousand and four thousand dollars. He handled the usual property transfers, wills, adoptions, and *lawsuits*. He just didn't have enough paying cases to make a decent living. Thurgood never turned anyone away, especially if the case had to do with civil rights. Such cases involved the government or a person or institution treating African-Americans differently from whites. Thurgood went into court many times on behalf of African-American teachers. First they brought suit for pay equal to that of white teachers. They they sued again when they were fired for hiring a lawyer in the first place. Thurgood was also successful in de-segregating local public parks. And he filed and won another case that resulted in the opening of public golf courses to all people, regardless of color.

In one of his early Baltimore civil rights cases, Thurgood defended the people who started the Pennsylvania Avenue *boycott*. A boycott is the refusal to shop in certain stores or to buy certain products. The boycott was started because African-Americans were upset with white-owned stores. The white shop-keepers were only too happy to sell merchandise to neighborhood blacks. But these same merchants re-fused to hire blacks to work in their stores. The peo-ple protested with a boycott. Boycotts happen to be as old as America. But the local shopkeepers forgot their history. They forgot that boycotts were used as far back as colonial times, when American patriots strug-gled against British power.

The shopkeepers went to court against the group that started the boycott, the National Association for the Advancement of Colored People. That organiza-tion, usually called by its initials *NAACP*, was founded in 1909 to promote the rights of African-Americans. The merchants' lawyers told the judge that the boycott was illegal. They even tried to argue that the law required blacks to shop in their neighborhood stores. Thurgood did a great deal of legal research on the case, spending hours in the local library. He read what other judges had ruled in similar situations. In court, Charles Houston joined his former student to argue the boycotters' side.

The court agreed with Houston and Thurgood. The judge's decision stated that black customers had the right not to shop in certain stores if they didn't like the storekeepers' hiring practices.

By the mid 1930s, Charles Houston had gone to work with the NAACP headquarters in New York City. The organization wanted Congress to pass laws protecting African-Americans' rights. But NAACP lawyers had more success when they went to court. There they could argue powerfully against laws already in existence.

Charles Houston believed strongly in Thurgood's abilities as an attorney. He recommended Thurgood for just about every NAACP lawsuit filed in the Baltimore area. Fighting civil rights battles brought Thurgood many clients—but little money. The NAACP was not a rich organization. It depended on donations for its income. But most of the members were black, and many African-Americans were poor or had only modest incomes. The NAACP was able to pay Thurgood only for his expenses. He contributed his legal talents and court time free of charge.

In 1935, Houston asked Thurgood if he'd like to join in a lawsuit to desegregate the University of Maryland Law School. Houston really didn't need to ask. He knew about Thurgood's rejected application to the school. And he knew that the memory of that rejection still made Thurgood angry. Thurgood jumped at the chance to work on the case.

The *plaintiff*, the person bringing the lawsuit, was Donald Gaines Murray. He was an African-American man who had graduated with honors from Amherst College. Now he was asking the court to order the University of Maryland to admit him to its law school. Just as the University of Maryland had turned down Thurgood, it now would not accept Murray.

According to *Plessy v. Ferguson,* a 1896 Supreme Court case, it was legal for a state or city to separate white and black people. There was only one requirement. If the city or state provided something for whites—a drinking fountain, for instance—it had to provide the same thing for blacks as well. The wording in the court decision was "separate but equal." In the case of the University of Maryland Law School, there was no equal law school for African-Americans available in that state. If Mr. Murray wanted to attend law school, it would have to be in another state. Maryland had no law school for blacks. This was the same argument the university had given Thurgood when he had applied.

The NAACP filed court papers for Mr. Murray in April 1935. On the day the hearing opened, June 18, Buster was in court. So were Thurgood's parents. And so was the press. In fact, the whole state of Maryland was in an uproar over the Murray case. Because of the great interest in it, Thurgood worked hard on preparing the case. He would be at his best.

39

Charles Houston was the chief attorney in court, but Thurgood took an active part in questioning the witnesses. He also made the *closing statement*. In it, Thurgood summed up the case, then gave the judge a strong reason for ruling in favor of Mr. Murray. He told Judge Eugene O'Dunne that the case was not only about the rights of his client. It also was about "the moral commitment stated in our country's creed."

On June 25, Judge O'Dunne ordered the University of Maryland Law School to immediately admit Donald Murray. Thurgood's keen and careful arguments had won an important victory for civil rights. But winning this case gave Thurgood a good feeling for another reason, too. "It was sweet revenge," he said later, recalling his own rejection from the university just five years before.

# Matters of Life and Death

When the NAACP won its case against the University of Maryland Law School, Charles Houston knew he'd been right in placing his faith in Thurgood's ability. Thurgood Marshall was a winner. And a winner was exactly what the NAACP needed at its national office in New York City. It was in the New York office that major decisions were made about how the NAACP would fight racial injustice all over the United States.

In 1936, Houston offered Thurgood the position of assistant special counsel for the NAACP. The job would make Thurgood the number two lawyer in the legal department, the NAACP's most important department. Thurgood's annual salary would be $2,400. "I don't know of anybody I would rather have in the office than you," Houston wrote to Thurgood, "or anybody who can do a better job of research and preparation of cases."

It was "the break of my lifetime," Thurgood said later. "I felt that I suddenly had a real chance to do something to end Jim Crow." Thurgood would now be able to use his legal education full-time to challenge the South's segregation laws.

Thurgood and Buster packed their few belongings

and headed for New York. But Thurgood traveled a lot in his new job. Many of the cases he handled began in the South. Thurgood commuted back and forth between the NAACP headquarters at 69 Fifth Avenue in New York City and the small office he still had in Baltimore. He also kept returning to Baltimore "to take care of the clients that really need me until they adjusted over to new lawyers."

Thurgood and Charles Houston believed they had a winning formula in the way they had won the Maryland law school case. They decided to use the same method in future cases. The directors of the NAACP believed the time was right for smashing Jim Crow laws in two other areas of adult education. First, the NAACP would sue professional schools, those that trained doctors and lawyers. Second, it would sue segregated graduate schools. These were schools that awarded advanced college degrees and trained professors. Thurgood Marshall believed that such professional schools should not admit, or turn down, people because of their race.

A main goal of the NAACP was to destroy barriers to higher education. But the NAACP helped blacks with other problems, too. A young man might be unjustly accused of a crime. Or a contract dispute might come up. Or a person might be turned away when trying to register to vote. All of these cases came to the NAACP.

Once Thurgood became a full-time civil rights lawyer, his reputation grew. He was always the first one that a local NAACP asked for. "Thurgood is coming!" would spread along the grapevine in troubled African-

American neighborhoods. The news brought with it a glimmer of hope. Thurgood, people believed, would win. But his success in winning so many cases was only part of the reason for his popularity. The other reason was his ability to be equally at home with all people. Though he himself was educated and polished, he was not too stuffy to talk to country people or those who lived on the street. He could play a hand of cards, could cuss and talk slang with the best of them.

"He could sit in the barbershop and talk like he was one of the U Street boys," Gardner Bishop told a reporter. Bishop was Thurgood's barber in Washington and a good friend. "But everybody in the shop, even my shoeshine boy, knew Thurgood could speak perfect English, and did when he took a case to court."

To do his work, Thurgood traveled throughout the South in a beat-up 1929 Model T Ford. "You have to understand that we had absolutely no money in those days," he said later. "Charlie [Houston] would sit in my car and type out the briefs.... We'd stay at friends' homes in those days—for free, you understand."

In 1941, Thurgood received a frantic call from someone in Hugo, Oklahoma, asking for legal help. It was on behalf of a twenty-one-year-old African-American handyman by the name of W. D. Lyons. The man was charged with killing three whites, a man and woman and their four-year-old son. Lyons was also accused of setting fire to the victims' house to cover up his crime.

Following his arrest, W. D. had been held in jail for eleven days without being allowed to talk to a lawyer.

He was beaten with an iron pipe and was not permitted to sleep. The police tried to weaken Lyons even more by not feeding him the usual three meals a day. Nor did they allow him to go to the bathroom. They even showed him Oklahoma's electric chair, and described how a condemned man was strapped in before the switch was thrown.

But in spite of the *third degree*, as such cruel treatment was called in those days, W. D. kept insisting that he was innocent. That only angered the police more. They wouldn't let him go. They wanted to make what they called a "good arrest," an arrest complete with a confession.

That's when the police brought out the pan of bones.

W. D. was exhausted. Beaten and questioned repeatedly, he sat slumped in his chair. A police officer put the pie pan filled with bone fragments in Lyons's lap. The officer told him that these charred bones were all that remained of the murdered parents and their young son.

W. D. was a poorly educated man. He also was superstitious. All his life he had been scared to death of anything having to do with ghosts. W. D. took one look at the pan of bones and screamed in terror. He flung the horrid objects off his lap. As the metal pan clattered to the floor, Lyons begged the police to take the bones away.

The police officers got their way. Terrified, Lyons broke down and agreed to sign a confession.

Thurgood knew the odds were heavily against W. D. Lyons. But he couldn't leave the frightened young man to face his trial alone. Nor could he leave him with a local attorney who didn't believe W. D. was innocent. Thurgood notified the prisoner's family that he would take the case.

Just as Thurgood feared, the signed confession made it impossible to convince a jury of Lyons's innocence. In presenting W. D.'s defense, Thurgood exposed a plot by local criminals to blame the crime on W. D. It turned out that the murdered man and his wife had been selling alcohol. This was against the law in that part of Oklahoma at that time. Thurgood carefully outlined how the two adults had been killed by a hit man, someone hired to commit the murder. Then their young son died when he was trapped in the fire. Thurgood also pointed out that the iron pipe used to beat W. D. was kept in the jail for use on every black person brought in for questioning.

The jury, however, was not convinced by Thurgood's arguments. W. D. was found guilty and sentenced to life in prison. In view of the racial hatred in that Oklahoma town, Thurgood considered it a victory that Lyons didn't get the death penalty.

Although the sentencing was unjust, Thurgood assured W. D. that he would keep on fighting. Thurgood filed an *appeal*—he asked the next higher court—for a new trial. But the Criminal Court of Appeals of Oklahoma denied this request. Then, in 1944, the *U.S. Supreme Court* dashed W. D.'s hopes for either an early release or a new trial. The court voted 6 to 3 that the confession used to convict Lyons was proper even though the police had obtained it through what the justices called "mistreatments."

For more than a decade after the trial, Thurgood sent small amounts of money to W. D. Thurgood hoped Lyons would realize he was not forgotten. Perhaps this remembrance would make the gross injustice a bit more tolerable to W. D.

W. D. was pardoned in 1965. Both historians and reporters have tried to locate him, but never had any success. W. D. Lyons just walked out of prison and disappeared.

From the Lyons case and the many others he tried, Thurgood Marshall learned a harsh lesson. He learned first-hand that many white Southerners had absolutely no respect for blacks, himself included. It made no difference that he was a graduate of one of the best law schools in the country. To white Southerners, Thurgood was viewed as an outside troublemaker. There were times when his life was in danger.

Thurgood was particularly watchful of the Ku Klux Klan. Its members, mostly poor and poorly educated young white men, believed in what they called *white supremacy*. The idea behind white supremacy was that white people should control all government offices. Then they would use their power to make laws that favored whites and put down blacks. The Ku Klux Klan demanded the complete segregation of whites and blacks. Klansmen also hated foreigners, Jews, and Catholics. Many of the cases Thurgood took were tried in small-town courtrooms. And it was in these small Southern towns that the Klan had its largest membership. The least the Klansmen were likely to do was to try to run Thurgood out of town. But it was not at all unheard of for the Klan to be more violent.

46

During the years Thurgood Marshall traveled through the South, the Klan beat many blacks, burned their homes, took their jobs away, and even killed some of them.

In his travels, Thurgood was unwelcome at white hotels because of the Jim Crow laws. Instead, he stayed with African-American families in their own homes. Sometimes, when there were rumors of trouble, he'd stay with one family one night, another the next. Often Thurgood changed cars as he moved about town, to confuse any Klansmen who might be following him. Then there were times when he'd walk through someone's front door, then sneak out the back, briefcase still in one hand, his suitcase in the other. This trick threw the Klansmen on the prowl off his trail. Local blacks even posted a watch outside the homes where Thurgood stayed. To let the neighbors know they needed guards, they circulated coded messages throughout the black community. Men were needed, the message said, "to sit up all night with a sick friend."

But all of these security measures didn't stop the threats that came in from many sides. The chief of police in Dallas once used racial insults when referring to Thurgood. He then told the police force that the next time Thurgood Marshall came to town, he "would personally" beat him up. The chief did not follow through even though he later came face-to-face with the civil rights lawyer. He used yet more racist language, and demanded that Thurgood "stay out of here."

In November 1946, Thurgood was in Columbia,

Tennessee. He had served as the attorney for two young men who had been arrested during a race riot in the town. The riot began when a black woman complained to a white radio repairman about the poor job he'd done fixing her radio. The white man slapped her. James Stephenson, the woman's nineteen-year-old son, who was also a Navy veteran, was with his mother in the shop. When he saw what the repairman had done, he punched the white man, knocking him through the shop's front window. Within minutes, the whole town had heard about the incident.

The sheriff arrested Stephenson and his mother. The repairman was only questioned. The Stephensons were eventually released on $3,500 bond, but this infuriated some local young white toughs. They gathered in a mob outside the jail. While the sheriff protected himself and his jail with a gun, the white mob turned its attention to the black community. Over the next several days, they burned, looted, and destroyed black-owned homes and businesses. Two blacks were killed. Twenty-five blacks, but only four whites, were arrested.

It was into a still-tense Columbia that Thurgood came to argue on behalf of the last two black men who had been arrested in the riot. Alexander Looby, a NAACP lawyer from Nashville, came with Thurgood. The attorneys managed to get one of the men freed. The other was given a five-year sentence. The police were angered by what they considered mild verdicts.

Looby, a local black man named Milton Murray, and several other black residents offered to accompany Thurgood when he left town. They wanted to be sure he got out safely. When Thurgood got into his car to drive away, he glanced in his rearview mirror. He saw a number of police cars following him. As he passed beyond the city limits, the police signaled him to pull over.

Thurgood stopped. He was ordered to get out and raise his hands. Looby and the others got out of the car, too.

The police told Thurgood they had a warrant to search his car. While one officer looked through the car, another arrested Thurgood. But instead of taking him into custody, several officers grabbed him roughly. They hustled him away from the road, down toward the banks of the Duck River. As they approached the water's edge, Thurgood saw a group of whites, including several state troopers, waiting in a small clearing. One of the troopers was holding a rope.

It was a lynch mob. They had planned the whole thing. They were going to hang Thurgood!

Looby and the others followed Thurgood's captors. When members of the mob looked back toward the road, they saw Looby and the other local black men watching them. Realizing there would be witnesses to any violence against Thurgood, the whites decided to let him go. Looby and the black men from Columbia had saved his life, Thurgood believed. After he and Looby drove farther away from town, the white mob pounced on the local blacks, including Milton Murray. The presence of the black men had prevented the lynching, and they would pay for it. One of the men was beaten so badly that he had to stay in the hospital for a month.

Did blacks in Columbia think Thurgood's visit to their town was worth the risk and the trouble? "Until Marshall came," Milton Murray said, "the law in Columbia was whatever a white lawyer or white policeman or white judge said it was. I admired . . . the willingness of this man to come into a race-crazy community and risk his life."

Thurgood argued the overwhelming number of his cases in Southern courtrooms. And it was in the deep South that his life was most often in danger. But there were areas in the North, too, where race problems had to be met and solved. In the late 1940s, the NAACP received complaints from blacks in Freeport, Long Island. They were being harassed, annoyed repeatedly, by Klansmen. These Klansmen, Thurgood was told, were also members of the local police department.

Despite warnings to stay out of town, Thurgood drove to Freeport. He parked his car and walked around the black community. Knocking on doors, Thurgood introduced himself and explained why he was there. As a result of his efforts, he gathered a number of sworn *affidavits*. An affidavit is a statement from a person saying exactly what happened to him or her. Thurgood would be able to use these affidavits in court.

When Thurgood got back to NAACP headquarters in New York City, he could report that nothing violent or illegal had been done to him. Thurgood had, however, noticed some hostile stares. And several other people had made rude comments. But based on what the Freeport African-Americans had told him,

Thurgood felt he was lucky to get in and out of town without an incident.

Thurgood went ahead and filed an official complaint with the state's attorney. Fortunately for the black residents of Freeport, the harassment stopped after Thurgood's visit.

Years later, whenever Thurgood looked back on his travels for the NAACP, he was reminded of the dangers he faced. But he always added, "You forget just one little . . . thing. I go into these places and I come out, on the fastest vehicle moving. The brave blacks are the ones who have to live there after I leave."

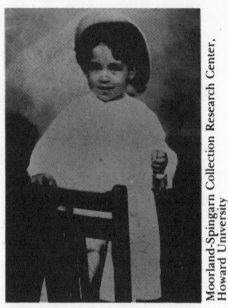

*In 1909 Thurgood Marshall turned one year old. He was named after his grandfather, Thorough Good Marshall.*

*Thurgood at two years of age.*

*Thurgood Marshall as a student at Frederick Douglass High School in Baltimore.*

*In 1936 Thurgood Marshall joined the NAACP as special counsel. He spent twenty-five years as a civil rights lawyer with the NAACP.*

*Thurgood Marshall's parents, Norma and William Marshall, in their home in Baltimore. They proudly display a photograph of their son Thurgood.*

*From left to right, George E. C. Hayes, Thurgood Marshall, and James Nabrit, Jr., stand outside the Supreme Court, May 17, 1954. Moments earlier the Court ruled in favor of the three attorneys' argument to end school segregation in the famous case of* **Brown v. Board of Education.**

*Thurgood's first wife, Vivian "Buster" Marshall. They were married for twenty-five years, until Vivian died, in 1955.*

*In 1961 Thurgood Marshall was sworn in by Judge J. Edward Lumbard as a judge in the U.S. Court of Appeals. Marshall was the first black to be appointed to the position by President John F. Kennedy.*

*During the 1960s, Thurgood Marshall helped colonies in Africa win freedom from European rule. Marshall helped write a constitution for Kenya, and he was President Kennedy's personal representative to Sierra Leone.*

*Thurgood Marshall with his second wife, Cecilia "Cissy" Suyat, and their two children, Thurgood junior (right) and John William.*

*Thurgood Marshall stands with President Lyndon B. Johnson as he nominates Thurgood to the Supreme Court.*

Harris and Ewing/Collection of
the Supreme Court of the United States

*Members of the Supreme Court pose for an official photo in
1967, the year Thurgood Marshall joined the Court. Thurgood
became the first African-American to serve on the Supreme
Court. He is in the back row, far right.*

Henry Grossman/*Life* Magazine © Time Warner

*Thurgood, Cissy Marshall, and their sons in front of the
Supreme Court. Cissy was proud of Thurgood's achievements
and provided him with a stable, happy home life.*

Thurgood announces his retirement from the Supreme Court in 1991, just before his eighty-third birthday.

*Thurgood enjoys the company of his grandson at his home in Falls Church, Virginia, in 1991. Thurgood Marshall died two years later, on January 24, 1993.*

# Winning the Right
# to Vote

Lonnie Smith is not a famous name. But even though few people have ever heard of him, this black dentist made history.

In 1940, Dr. Smith tried to vote in the Texas *primary election*. In a primary election, or primary, a party choses candidates who will run for office. But the election judge, S. C. Allwright, refused to give Dr. Smith a ballot. Smith told the judge there must be some mistake. The dentist showed the election officials his *poll tax* receipt. The slip of paper meant he had paid his voting tax. That entitled him to vote. But the judge still refused to give him a ballot.

Dr. Smith was furious. He talked the matter over with his local NAACP. Dr. Smith then decided to sue the election officials in Harris County, the place where he lived. He believed that the Fifteenth Amendment to the U.S. Constitution gave him the right to vote.

The Fifteenth Amendment had been introduced into Congress in February 1869. The following year, it was ratified by the necessary three-fourths of the states. The amendment was added to the Constitution to guarantee the vote to former slaves. The voting rights of former slaves in the South were threatened by the newly formed Ku Klux Klan. The Fifteenth Amendment says that no citizen may be denied the right to vote "on account of race, color, or previous condition of servitude." Servitude meant slavery.

The Fifteenth Amendment should have settled the voting rights issue, but it didn't. After the Civil War ended, the southern states were occupied by *Union* troops for years. Still, nothing was done to enforce black voting rights. Then, in 1877, President Rutherford B. Hayes pulled the federal troops out of the South. This action turned the state governments back over to the native white Southerners. Once the whites were in charge again, they passed laws limiting the number of blacks who could vote. For instance, one law required a voter to show election officials that he could read and write. Whites were allowed to demonstrate this by just writing their names. But when an African-American wanted to register, he was required to read a portion of the state constitution. Such tests, called literacy tests, were meant to show how well a person could read. Some states added another requirement to these tests. Not only did the person have to read some part of the state's constitution, he had to explain what it meant. Explaining what any constitution means is not easy. Even simple laws can be hard to explain. The language can be complicated and can be understood in different ways. That is why so many lawsuits are filed. Opposing sides have to ask a third party, a judge, to settle the argument over exactly what the law says.

In states with literacy tests, black citizens were not

very successful in registering to vote. The few who tried found that the voting officials always ruled against them. Sometimes even African-Americans with masters degrees from well-known universities were rejected. They were told simply they could not properly read and explain their state's constitution.

Some southern states had another way to keep black people from voting. Like Texas, those states required voters to pay a tax before they could vote. It was called a poll tax. Voters paid it when they registered. But many poor blacks couldn't afford the poll tax. That meant they couldn't vote.

After the 1880s, yet another method was used by Southern states to control who registered. It was called the grandfather clause. This law stated that if your grandfather voted in the election of 1860, you, too, could register to vote. But the overwhelming majority of African-American men living in the South in 1860 were still slaves. They weren't permitted to vote. Under the grandfather clause, neither were the grandchildren of those nineteenth-century blacks permitted to register and vote.

Why did southern whites keep African-Americans from voting? There is probably no single reason. One of the most likely explanations is that the whites were afraid of losing their power to run everything. There were many counties in the South where blacks outnumbered whites. If the blacks could vote, what would stop them from electing African-American officials? At the very least, they might vote out of office those whites who didn't treat blacks fairly.

Another reason was that most white people in the

South were Democrats in those days. If African-Americans had been allowed to vote, historians believed that they probably would have supported the *Republican party*. After all, the Republican party was the party of Abraham Lincoln. He was the president who signed the *Emancipation Proclamation,* which freed the slaves. White people believed that their power depended on keeping blacks from voting. And white people freely used both violence and Jim Crow laws to keep African-Americans from the ballot box.

The *Democratic party* of Texas claimed it was a private club. For that reason, its members said, the party's primary election was a private activity. Of course, no African-Americans were allowed to be members of this private club. As a result, not a single black could vote in the primary. The primary even was known locally as the White Primary.

When Dr. Smith decided to press his case, the local Harris County NAACP contacted the national office. Thurgood Marshall was assigned to the case. Thurgood read Dr. Smith's statement about trying to vote, and immediately filed suit in the federal district court in Houston, Texas. Thurgood argued his case before Judge T. M. Kennerly. He said that the right to vote was guaranteed by the Fifteenth Amendment. Any law or trick aimed at turning away a qualified black voter was *unconstitutional,* not allowed by the Constitution.

Judge Kennerly listened politely to Thurgood—then dismissed the case in May 1942. When a judge dismisses a case, it means he will not hear it. In other words, Thurgood lost. Thurgood then took the case to the next higher court, the *U.S. Court of Appeals*. It, too, ruled against him. At that point, there was only one court left to go to. Thurgood took his case to the U.S. Supreme Court in Washington, D.C.

In 1944, in the case known as *Smith v. Allwright*, the Supreme Court agreed with Thurgood. Dr. Smith's rights had been denied when Judge Allwright told Smith he could not vote. The Democrats' all-white primary was declared unconstitutional. Further, the court said that all African-Americans in Texas should be registered to vote not just in primaries, but in *general elections* as well.

Winning the *Smith v. Allwright* case was a major victory. But the battle to win respect for African-Americans' right to vote was not over. As a result of the Court decision, more blacks did register and vote. But thousands still were fearful. They worried that the Ku Klux Klan would terrorize them if they tried to vote. It would not be until 1965, ninety-five years after the Fifteenth Amendment was passed, that Congress would finally come forth with a strong voting rights law.

Thurgood had every reason to be proud of his work in winning the *Smith* case. He had tested his legal skills before the highest court in the land. Clearly, he was one of the best lawyers in the country—though he was far from the richest. The NAACP was not able to reward its most successful attorney with a bonus or a high salary. The organization did, however, recognize his work by giving him an important honor. In 1946, the NAACP awarded Thurgood the Spingarn Medal. The award was named after Arthur B. Spingarn, a dedicated white lawyer who had served as chief attorney for the NAACP. Spingarn had taken the job in 1914, more than thirty years earlier. In those days, the NAACP's legal department spent most of its time and energy fighting violence against blacks. By the middle of the twentieth century, the issues facing blacks might have changed. But with Thurgood fighting for African-Americans' rights, the struggle continued to be in good hands.

Thurgood was moved by the award. It was the highest honor the NAACP could bestow.

# The Right to an Equal Education

Thurgood Marshall knew that if a person was to grow up to be a success, that person needed a good education. But as America reached the middle of the twentieth century, such an education was not available to African-American children. They had to go to schools for blacks only. These schools for blacks, though separate from whites, were supposed to be as good as schools attended by whites. But that was hardly the case. Why was education for black children still in such a terrible state? The answer goes back to the 1896 Supreme Court decision known as *Plessy v. Ferguson.*

In *Plessy v. Ferguson,* the Supreme Court ruled that Southern states could segregate black citizens from whites so long as the separate facilities—schools, parks, waiting rooms, water fountains—were equal. This meant if there was a library in a local white school, the local black school should have an equal library. The same was true for an auditorium, science lab, art room, even a football stadium for a high school. Whatever facilities the school board provided in white schools were also supposed to be provided in black schools.

That was the law.

What really existed was something else. In a 1937 book, sociologist John Dollard wrote about life in Southern Town. That was a made-up name for a small town somewhere in the deep South. Dollard pointed out that the local board of education had "great reluctance" to spend money on African-American schools. If blacks wanted heat in their school buildings during cold weather, the black community had to collect money for coal or firewood. Then they had to go out and buy it themselves. The school board wouldn't even provide basic school equipment. Black teachers had to buy chalk, maps, and paper with their own money if their students were to have such supplies.

In Mississippi, black elementary-school children were given worn-out, hand-me-down textbooks from white schools. Even those came only after the white schools ordered and received brand-new books. In both Florida and North Carolina, textbooks couldn't be handed down. They had to be kept entirely separate. In those states, black students didn't even get a chance to see the books used by white students.

In his book, Dollard interviewed a number of white citizens in Southern Town. They told him that the local "Negroes," as black people were then called, should be happy with their high school. The whites held this opinion even though the black high school offered only three years of classes, instead of the usual four. Nor did the school offer all the required high-school courses. The school year itself was shorter for blacks than for whites. And less time in school meant less education. Because African-American students were mostly the children of tenant farmers—who farmed land owned by someone else—they had to help their parents bring in the crops during harvest season. White landowners told their black tenants that if the children didn't work in the fields, the black family would be asked to move. Black parents didn't have a choice. They had to make their children work in the fields because they supported themselves by farming. Black children seldom started classes until November. For white children, school opened a month earlier.

And when African-American children did report to school, quite often the classes weren't even held in a school building. Churches often served as houses of worship on Sundays, then were used as schools during the week.

Throughout the South, salaries for all teachers were the lowest in the nation. And they were lowest of all for black teachers. Still, white educators in the South were paid three times more than black teachers.

African-Americans resented the gross difference between the two sets of schools. Harry Briggs, Sr., was no exception. By 1950, he and his wife, Liza, were angry, too; angry enough to be willing to do something about it. Briggs worked at a gas station in Summerton, South Carolina. During World War II, he joined the Navy and served in the South Pacific. He

68

and Liza, who worked at a local motel, wanted a better life for their son.

Harry Briggs, Jr., attended an all-black school run by the board of education in Clarendon County. The building was in terrible condition. On rainy days the roof leaked. And even though the white children rode to school on a bus, there was no bus assigned to young Harry or to any of the other black students. They had to walk to school.

At first, Harry and Liza simply wanted the school board to live up to the law. They wanted equal facilities. They wanted a building that was as good as the whites' school. They also wanted buses to pick up and return the black children to their neighborhoods every day. But the more the Briggs thought about it, the more they wanted an end to segregation itself. They wanted Harry, Jr., along with all of the other students in Clarendon County, both black and white, to attend the same public schools.

Harry and Liza knew they were asking for trouble. The man from the local NAACP warned them. In the past, whenever a black person had filed suit against the white-dominated government, something bad had happened. And the NAACP was right this time, too. Both Harry and Liza lost their jobs when they refused to drop their lawsuit.

Thurgood and the other NAACP lawyers had serious discussions—and disagreements—over how to handle the Clarendon County case. Thurgood had handled many civil rights cases for the NAACP. In them, his argument always had been that the state was wrong. It was wrong because it was not providing equal facilities, opportunities, or schools for African-Americans. The major reason he won the University of Maryland Law School case was that the state of Maryland had not provided a separate and equal law school for blacks. This was a clear violation of the *Plessy* decision, which said that blacks could be separated from whites if they were given their own, equal schools.

Thurgood knew the safe way to handle the Briggs's suit would be to ask for equal schools. It would be fairly easy to prove in court that South Carolina was not living up to the "equal" part of the *Plessy* decision. And Thurgood believed that when school officials and legislators in that state were faced with a lawsuit, they would probably agree to improve African-American schools. They would do that in hopes of stopping the growing calls for integration. Integration meant that black students would go to white schools, and that's what many Southern whites feared most. Thurgood worried that white people would try to stop integration at all costs.

For this reason, Thurgood knew that asking the court for integration was very risky. Many people in the NAACP, and in the black community as a whole, believed that if they asked for a complete end to separate schools, they would lose. And if they lost, it could be another hundred years before the dream of full equality might again become a possibility. Some argued that equal schools, even if they were separate, would be better than the poor schools black children now had.

70

Thurgood wanted to advance the cause of his people, but he also wanted to win. He thought very hard for days. Finally, against the advice of friends and colleagues, Thurgood decided to take a chance. He would sue for integration of schools, not just for equal schools. It was time African-Americans became first-class citizens. "We want no more [than that]," he announced. "We will not take less," he added.

In his case, Thurgood would ask the court to overturn the *Plessy* "separate but equal" decision. Thurgood believed that there was no such thing as "separate but equal." When you separate people, it can only be because one group is not respected as much as the other. If that is the case, even if a school for blacks looks exactly like a school for whites, how could the two groups of students ever be thought of as equal?

When Thurgood prepared for this case, he wrote a *brief* that was carefully thought out. A brief is a detailed essay written by a lawyer to present his side of a case. In his brief, Thurgood stated that the separation of white and black students into different schools creates a sense of superiority in one group, and inferiority in the other. Dr. Kenneth Clark, a well-known African-American psychologist, helped Thurgood develop his ideas. The psychologist had studied the effects of segregation on black children.

Dr. Clark drew his conclusions from what is known as his "doll study." One at a time, young African-American schoolchildren were brought into a room. A brown doll and a white one lay on a table before them. Each child was asked to point to the doll that looked most like him or her. The next question was, Which doll is the good doll? Finally, each child was asked, Which doll is the bad doll? Dr. Clark kept a careful tally of which dolls each child pointed to.

Dr. Clark found that the African-American children picked the brown doll as looking most like themselves. But when it came to choosing the good doll, the results were very troublesome. Most of the African-American children pointed to the white doll. And when directed to select the bad doll, they pointed to the brown one. The study gave evidence that African-American children thought that white was good and brown was bad. Dr. Clark concluded that African-American children had a poor view of themselves. He believed this poor self-image was learned in segregated schools in segregated communities.

In addition to Dr. Clark's assistance, Thurgood had the help of many other experts. There were civil rights lawyers from Howard University and several black historians. A number of white experts helped as well. One of them was Jack Greenberg, an attorney who was Thurgood's deputy, assisting him in his work. Another was Alfred H. Kelly, a historian from Wayne State University in Detroit, Michigan. The brief that Thurgood finally prepared was thorough and impressive. And it was truly the result of a team of blacks and whites working closely together.

Thurgood's argument was based on the Fourteenth Amendment. It says that no state may "deny to any person within its jurisdiction the equal protection of the laws." Thurgood was prepared to argue that when blacks and whites were separated in different schools, they were not receiving the "equal protection of the laws." They were not receiving what they were due.

The case, known as *Briggs v. Elliot*, was first tried in the South Carolina District Court, before a three-judge panel. In order to win, Thurgood needed at least two of the three judges to vote for his side. Although he had spent hours preparing his case, privately Thurgood did not expect to win at the state level.

And he did not.

One of the three judges, however, disagreed with his two colleagues. He supported Thurgood's argument. Segregation in education, Judge Waring announced from the bench, "can never produce equality. . . ." And, he added, it is "an evil that must be eradicated."

Court adjourned in an uproar as reporters raced out to phone their newspapers with the court's decision. Thurgood gathered his law books and legal papers and put them back into his briefcase. This stage of the case might be over, but Thurgood knew it was just the opening battle.

Some people working on the case were disappointed that they had not won. But Thurgood understood that losing at this early stage did not mean the end of the matter. All along, NAACP attorneys figured they would have to take the fight to a higher court. Within days of the *Briggs* decision, Thurgood filed an appeal with the United States Supreme Court.

The case that Thurgood filed with the Supreme Court is known as *Brown v. Board of Education*. In fact, it was a bundle of five lawsuits filed by plaintiffs living

73

in different states and the District of Columbia. Harry Briggs's suit was included in the *Brown* case. But it was Linda Brown who gave the case its name.

Linda Brown lived in Topeka, Kansas. She was a seven-year-old African-American girl. Her father, the Reverend Oliver Brown, had tried to enroll Linda in the all-white school that was only four blocks from their home. He was told the school would not accept her. The school official said Linda would have to travel nearly two miles to the school for blacks. The board of education provided bus transportation, but Linda would have to walk six blocks, along dangerous railroad tracks, to get to the bus stop.

The other three plaintiffs in the case came from Virginia, Delaware, and Washington, D.C. The cases of the five plaintiffs weren't exactly alike, but they all had one thing in common. The issue was whether separate schools were acceptable under the Fourteenth Amendment.

The Supreme Court set Tuesday, December 9, 1952, as the day the justices would listen to the *oral arguments*. Oral arguments are short speeches made by the lawyers on both sides of the case.

Several weeks earlier, the court had received briefs from lawyers for the defense. The defense—or *defendant*—is the person or group being sued. In the *Brown* case, the defense was made up of the school systems that wouldn't allow the black plaintiffs to attend white schools. The defense wanted to keep the laws that had set up segregated schools. It didn't want Harry Briggs, Jr., Linda Brown, or the other African-American children to attend white schools.

At the same time that the defendants submitted briefs, the plaintiffs, those bringing the suit, presented their own brief to the nine justices. In it, Thurgood claimed that the plaintiffs, the young black students, were being denied their constitutional rights. They were not allowed to attend white schools. The NAACP brief that Thurgood presented was long—235 printed pages. It was filled with complicated legal language and deep research about segregation.

Thurgood's turn to address the Supreme Court came on Wednesday, December 10. Over the years, he had stood before the justices many times. Still, this was the biggest case of his life. He was asking the Court to throw out a decision it had made in 1896. It is rare that the Supreme Court ever "reverses itself," or changes its mind. Thurgood had to admit he was scared.

"No matter how many times I argued there," he later said, "I never got used to it. Just the voice of the court crier could make your knees shake."

The court crier opened that session of the court in the usual way. "Oyez! Oyez! Oyez!" he called. *Oyez,* pronounced oh-yay, is an old word that means "Hear ye!" Then the crier continued, "All persons having business before the Honorable, the Supreme Court of the United States, are invited to draw near and give their attention, for the Court is now sitting. God save the United States and this Honorable Court."

Thurgood may have been nervous on the inside, but when he rose to address the Court that day, his voice was steady and his arguments were strong. At times he was formal in his speech. Other times, he spoke in a homespun, down-to-earth style. He tried to use common sense in his arguments. He asked the justices to put themselves in the shoes of his clients. What would *they* want if they were in the same situation?

As Thurgood made his arguments that morning, he started to get a sinking feeling. The justices kept interrupting him to ask questions. Such interruptions are not unusual in Court. But each attorney had only thirty minutes to make his best points. Thurgood felt himself being sidetracked. Every time he tried to make a tighter argument, he was asked to stop and explain something. It was distracting enough to be interrupted once. Thurgood's courtroom experience told him it was now happening too many times.

To win, Thurgood needed five of the nine justices to vote for his side. Thurgood left the courtroom feeling downcast. He sensed that the votes simply were not there, that he might lose.

The Supreme Court makes its decisions in secret, behind closed doors. A decision can take weeks to make. There is no secretary to take minutes, or official notes, and no other record is kept of the justices' discussions. It is rare that the public ever finds out what the justices said to one another or which arguments carried the most weight. Only after the justices have voted does the public learn who won. As the weeks dragged on, Thurgood wondered why the Court was taking so long to hand down a decision.

Thurgood finally learned why. The Court was divided. It was unable to reach a decision. The justices decided to call back the lawyers for both sides. The lawyers would be asked to give additional arguments.

Thurgood was thrilled. This meant he had a second chance.

At that time, history also stepped in to help Thurgood's cause. President Eisenhower appointed Earl Warren to replace Chief Justice Vinson, who had died suddenly of a heart attack. Earl Warren was on record as having said, "I insist upon one law for all men." It was to this new Chief Justice that Thurgood Marshall addressed his words in December 1953.

Thurgood argued that the Supreme Court could no longer uphold segregated schooling. If it did, the Court would be saying that blacks were inferior to all other races. What other reason could there be to separate them from white people? In addition, Thurgood argued, the Fourteenth Amendment does not allow such an action. Discrimination was contrary to the nation's stated ideals.

Thurgood felt encouraged when his speaking time was up. He had presented strong arguments, and he had put them in the language of justice and equality. That's what America was supposed to be all about.

In June 1954, the Supreme Court came to a decision. It ruled unanimously that "separate schools are inherently—by their very nature—unequal." Segregated schools were declared unconstitutional.

The ruling was one of the major Supreme Court decisions in American history. It was no less of a personal triumph for Thurgood Marshall.

# Mr. Civil Rights

Thurgood Marshall was back in Court less than a year following the *Brown* decision. This time he was arguing that school desegregation should take place immediately. He wanted the Court to set a specific date for Southern white schools to admit African-American students. When the Court finally ruled on the question, it gave no exact time schedule. The Court just said "with all deliberate speed." Still, the decision was another victory for Thurgood and the NAACP. They were one step closer to their goal of integration.

Sadly, Thurgood could not savor the victory. Late in 1954, he was told that his wife, Buster, had cancer. She had kept the news from him because she knew it would upset him. She wanted him to be able to concentrate on the school desegregation case. When Thurgood learned the truth about Buster's illness, he nearly collapsed.

Thurgood and Buster had been married for twenty-five years. They had shared many happy times, and sad ones, too. Thurgood and Buster had hoped to have a family, but never had any children. And they both had experienced much loneliness. Buster had stayed by herself in their New York apartment through the many long days and weeks that Thurgood was away trying cases. But she had never complained.

Now, with Buster lying sick in their apartment, Thurgood stayed home as much as he could. During her final days, Thurgood seldom went out. He cooked for his wife and fed her, read to her, and gave her her medicine.

Buster died quietly on February 11, 1955, her forty-fourth birthday.

"I thought my world had come to an end," Thurgood told a friend.

But the world did not stop—at least not forever. Thurgood grieved, then he turned again to work. He threw himself back into the struggle to gain full equality for African-Americans.

Because of his successes in court, Thurgood had become a celebrity. He was known as "Mr. Civil Rights" in black communities all over America. And he was sought after for interviews by magazine and newspaper reporters. *Newsweek* magazine interviewed Thurgood in 1956. He assured the reporter that the NAACP would not let up on its work. Whenever it ran "up against a brick wall," he said, the NAACP would keep on asking the courts to right the injustice.

But not only were readers given stories about Thurgood's legal victories, the public also learned details about the man himself. The press was eager to run stories about the famous lawyer. When Thurgood remarried, news of the wedding made the newspapers.

Thurgood's new bride was Cecilia Suyat, called "Cissy" for short. Of Filipino descent, Cissy had come to New York City from her native Hawaii in 1947. She found work as a secretary at the NAACP headquarters. It was there that she met Thurgood.

Cissy at first had plans of her own. She turned Thurgood down the first time he proposed. She told him that she wanted to train to become a court reporter.

Those who knew Thurgood at that time remember him as a polished, handsome man. "Women always wanted to get to know [him]," Ersa Poston, a friend, recalled. But by then, Thurgood had taken a fancy to the petite Cissy. He thought her both beautiful and charming, and he was persistent in asking her out on dates. When he asked her a second time to marry him, she agreed. The wedding took place in December 1955.

The match was a good one. Thurgood soon came to depend on Cissy's advice and judgment. "Cissy, like Buster, provided the support Thurgood needed," Ersa Poston commented. "She brought an order to his life." Like Buster, Cissy understood that she would be sharing her husband with the struggle for equal rights. Thurgood often worked long hours, and now more great change was in the air. By the mid-1950s, the United States was experiencing a revolution in civil rights. By that time, too, many homes had televisions. Americans could sit in their living rooms and see the news "live," as it happened, on their small screens. One of the big news stories of late 1955 was the beginning of a bus boycott in Montgomery, Alabama. The country watched.

The boycott started with Rosa Parks, a forty-two-year-old African-American woman. Rosa was on her way home from work one day. She was tired. Her feet ached, and every muscle in her body was sore. She had put in another hard day at work. Rosa was a seamstress for a department store in Montgomery. When a man bought a suit or coat that needed some adjustments, Rosa did the sewing. If a woman customer needed a hem raised or lowered on a new skirt, that, too, was Rosa's job.

The bus finally pulled up at the stop where Rosa had been waiting. She welcomed the opportunity to be able to sit down. She entered the bus and paid her ten-cent fare. Rosa took this bus every day so she recognized the driver. His name was J. F. Blake. He nodded, but he was not particularly friendly. Blake had a reputation for being rude and disrespectful to the black people who rode his bus.

Rosa saw there was a large selection of empty seats in the black section, the section in the back of the bus. The front ten rows of the buses always were reserved for white people.

Rosa took a seat in the first row of the black section. Three other blacks had boarded at the same time she did, and they sat down with her.

As the bus made its way through Montgomery, more blacks and whites boarded. Several stops later, the white section was filled. According to Alabama law, if there were no more seats available in the white section of the bus, black passengers could be asked to give up their seats so that the whites could sit down.

"You let them have those front seats," J. F. Blake told Rosa and the other blacks in her row.

Rosa didn't feel like standing. The other blacks hesitated. They didn't want to move any more than Rosa Parks did, but they knew what could happen if they didn't. They moved.

Rosa stayed in her seat.

The bus driver said, "Look, woman, I told you I wanted the seat. Are you going to stand up?"

Rosa Parks had not planned for this moment. She had not set out on the morning of December 1, 1955, to make history. She was just tired from work, too tired to move. She was also tired of the indignity that segregation had heaped upon her all her life.

"No," Rosa told the bus driver. She wasn't going to move.

J. F. Blake called the police. When the officers arrived, Rosa was still sitting in her seat. One of the officers asked her why she hadn't obeyed the bus driver. She told him she didn't think she should have to.

"Why do you push us around?" she asked the police.

News of Rosa's arrest spread quickly through Montgomery's black community. Friends posted bail so that Rosa didn't have to spend the night in jail.

Ed Nixon, head of the local NAACP, believed Rosa's arrest made a perfect case. It could be used to challenge the city's Jim Crow law separating bus riders on the basis of color. Nixon had another idea, too. He wanted to make the challenge double-fisted. The NAACP would sue the city for its policy on bus segregation. At the same time, the black community of Montgomery would boycott, refuse to ride, the buses.

If Montgomery's African-Americans organized properly, Nixon thought, the plan could work. After all, the majority of the bus company's customers were black. The bus company would lose thousands of dollars without their business. Nixon was betting the bus company couldn't afford that, and would be forced to change its segregation policy.

Thurgood took over the case. He filed suit in federal court, asking that Montgomery's buses be desegregated. At the same time, the African-American community organized the boycott. Thousands of flyers were distributed, urging blacks not to ride the buses. Instead, the black bus customers—more than 17,000 of them—were asked to walk to work or set up car pools.

The boycott was being led by a young clergyman. A newcomer from Atlanta, Georgia, he was pastor of the Dexter Avenue Baptist Church. His name was Martin Luther King, Jr. Under King's inspired leadership, the boycott was working. The bus company was losing a lot of money. If the protest continued, the company might be forced out of business. But Montgomery still didn't change its segregation policy. Instead, the police tried to disrupt the boycott. They arrested its leaders on any excuse they could find. If a taillight on a car-pool vehicle was burned out, the driver got a ticket. If a black pedestrian jaywalked, he might be taken downtown to the police station.

Events in Montgomery marked a major shift in the civil rights movement. Thurgood Marshall had always believed in working within the system, in doing things "peacefully, lawfully, and in the true American tradition." He did this by appealing to the courts for justice. He knew from experience that he had to choose his civil rights cases carefully. But if he did, and presented his arguments intelligently, the system would respond fairly. Sometimes, issues didn't get worked out immediately or the way he hoped. But he had faith that America would eventually be true to its belief that all men are created equal.

Martin Luther King, Jr.'s, group was using a different approach. They staged active protests, though the protests were a special kind. They were based on the idea of nonviolent civil disobedience. People would protest injustice, but never use violence, even if violence was being used against them. Martin Luther King had read the books of India's Mahatma Gandhi. That great leader had used nonviolent resistance to win his country's independence from the British. King believed the same tactics could work in the American South. With the boycott, he was learning that he was right.

Many NAACP old-timers did not approve of taking the fight for civil rights out of the courts. Public meetings, marches, and boycotts were not among the NAACP's weapons in the early days of the struggle for equal rights. For one thing, as Thurgood pointed out, protests and demonstrations got "people in jail." And he added, "We have to get them out." But it was equally clear to Thurgood that the NAACP could not stand on the sidelines as the civil rights movement changed. The NAACP became involved by raising money for the many boycotters' fines and their other expenses. The NAACP also provided the protesters with legal advice.

Meanwhile, the managers of the bus company knew that if the boycott didn't end soon, they would be out of business.

On November 13, nearly a year after the protest began, the U.S. Supreme Court ruled on Thurgood's suit. The court declared Montgomery's bus segregation law unconstitutional.

As a result of Dr. King's leadership and Thurgood's legal work, African-American bus riders, not only in Montgomery but all across the American South, could board a bus and sit in any available seat.

With John F. Kennedy's inauguration as president on January 20, 1961, there was a feeling of hope in the air. Many African-Americans believed they now had a man in the White House who truly understood their problems. And they believed he'd be willing to use the power of the nation's government to bring about better times for black people. After all, Kennedy had shown his support during his presidential campaign. When Martin Luther King, Jr., was sent to a Georgia prison, candidate Kennedy had used his influence to get King released.

African-Americans soon had a big reason to be hopeful. The Kennedy administration proposed a new civil rights law. It would guarantee blacks equal access to public accommodations. Public accommodations include theaters, restaurants, hotels and motels, train stations, airports, public rest rooms, and drinking fountains.

During the 1960s, African-Americans weren't the only blacks winning equality. Colonies in Africa itself were winning their freedom from European nations. Thurgood Marshall had become known around the world for his expert knowledge about law and civil rights. In 1961, he was invited to London to help write a constitution for Kenya. Kenya was a British colony in Africa. The Kenyans were about to gain their independence from England.

Soon afterward President Kennedy asked Thurgood to be his personal representative to Sierra Leone, another new African nation. Thurgood attended the independence ceremonies in that country.

Then, on September 23, 1961, President Kennedy nominated Thurgood to be a judge on the U.S. Court of Appeals for the Second Circuit. The Court of Appeals is sometimes called the circuit court. The Second Circuit includes New York, Connecticut, and Vermont. The Court of Appeals is a middle-level court in the federal court system. Most lawsuits with constitutional issues start at the lowest level, in the *U.S. District Court.* If either side in the case is not satisfied with that court's decision, that side can appeal—or ask—the court at the next level to hear the case. This next level is the Court of Appeals. If that court agrees to take the case, lawyers for both sides go to the court and argue for a new decision. The highest—and last—court in the United States is the Supreme Court, in Washington, D.C.

When Thurgood was nominated to the Court of Appeals, he hesitated before taking the job. He was concerned that he might only be a "token." That is, he might have been chosen because of his color, to please African-American people. And as a federal judge, he might not be able to do a great deal for civil rights. He wondered if he might be able to do more by staying on as the NAACP's chief lawyer. But Thurgood also had come to believe that the school desegregation decision in 1954 was his largest accomplishment. Perhaps it was for others to see that the decision was carried out.

"I've always felt the assault troops never occupy the town," he explained. "I figured after the school decisions, the assault was over for me." There now were other ways he could serve the cause of justice. And Thurgood was never one to turn down a challenge. Finally, he told President Kennedy he would serve.

During his four years as a judge on the Court of Appeals, Thurgood wrote ninety-eight *majority opinions*. A majority opinion is an essay written by one of the judges on the winning side in a case. In the essay, the judge explains which side won the lawsuit and why the court chose that side. Not one of Thurgood's opinions was ever reversed. That is, when any of his decisions were appealed to the next level, the Supreme Court, that Court never disagreed with Thurgood's opinions.

While Thurgood served on the Court of Appeals, he and Cissy continued to live in New York. By then they were parents. Thurgood junior had been born in 1959. John William arrived a year later. Thurgood enjoyed playing with the children, and spent as much time as he could with his young family.

# Supreme Court Justice

On June 13, 1967, President Lyndon Johnson phoned Thurgood Marshall and asked him to stop by the White House. The president told Thurgood he wanted to talk to him.

Thurgood had a pretty good idea of why the president might want to see him. A vacancy had opened up on the Supreme Court. There had been rumors that the president might nominate Thurgood to the position. In fact, Thurgood and Cissy had talked about the possibility just that morning.

When Thurgood arrived at the White House, he didn't want to appear over-confident. But the rumors proved correct. The president was offering him the position. Thurgood tried to act surprised when Lyndon Johnson told him the news. The president then wanted to know if Thurgood's wife knew of his nomination. Thurgood dodged the question. "How could she know?" he asked. After all, the president had only just made the offer.

The president wanted to suprise Mrs. Marshall. He ordered the White House switchboard to call her at home. The president then switched on the speakerphone.

Not knowing she was talking to both her husband

and Lyndon Johnson, Cissy immediately asked Thurgood about his meeting at the White House.

"Did you get the Supreme Court nomination?" she asked.

President Johnson burst out laughing. It obviously wasn't a surprise, after all.

Later, President Johnson said this to the nation, "I believe he earned that appointment, he deserves the appointment. He is best qualified. . . . I believe it is the right thing to do, the right time to do it, the right man and the right place."

Thurgood's entire life had prepared him for this moment. There were the many hours he'd spent in the courtrooms. There were the many history-making cases he had argued—and won. He had also received praise for his service on the Court of Appeals. And after four years on that court, Thurgood had advanced even further. In 1965, President Johnson had appointed Thurgood to the job of solicitor general of the United States. Thurgood was the nation's first African-American to hold that high office in the Department of Justice. The solicitor general is the government's main lawyer. It is the solicitor general who argues the government's side in cases before the Supreme Court. In working with the Supreme Court, the solicitor general also has office space in the Supreme Court building, and often discusses which appeals from the lower courts the Supreme Court justices might want to hear. The job of solicitor general, in fact, has long been a stepping-stone in a person's rise to the high court.

On October 1, 1967, Thurgood Marshall stood

proudly at the front of the Supreme Court chamber. He placed his left hand on a Bible that belonged to Justice Hugo Black. Thurgood and Hugo Black would now work together as justices on the Supreme Court. There was an important meaning in Thurgood's choice of that particular Bible. Years before in Alabama, Hugo Black had been a member of the Ku Klux Klan. Now he was a changed man. Thurgood believed that if one man could change, a nation could change as well, one person at a time.

Raising his right hand, Thurgood swore to "administer justice . . . and do equal right to the poor and to the rich."

Guests at this historic ceremony included Thurgood's wife, their two children, and his brother, Aubrey. Arthur Spingarn, one of the founders of the NAACP, was also sitting in the audience.

It had been the separation of black students from white in Southern schools that had provided Thurgood Marshall with the *Brown* case, the biggest of his career. But twenty years after Thurgood won that case, the issue of segregation was still before the Supreme Court. Some school systems kept putting off integration. Others tried voluntary plans. Many African-Americans were tired of waiting for school systems to do what they'd been ordered to do in 1954 and 1955. These people wanted action. Now Thurgood was a justice on the Supreme Court. He found himself in a position to be able to strike further blows at racial inequality in public schools.

While desegregation had moved slowly in the South, not much had been done about it in the North.

By the early 1970s, school segregation cases were coming from Northern school districts, too. The separation of black and white students in Northern public schools was not the result of Jim Crow laws. Instead, children in the North were usually assigned to the school in their own neighborhood. The problem was, most neighborhoods in Northern cities were either black or white. Boards of education could set up neighborhood boundaries in such a way as to assign the students from white neighborhoods to one school. All of the children from the black community would go to another school. Whenever the Supreme Court had a case that examined the way a Northern city assigned children to schools, Thurgood voted to desegregate. When desegregation could not be accomplished any other way, he pushed for busing. That meant transporting children to schools outside their neighborhood in order to make a more equal mix of black and white students. As a result, in cities all across the North, students were reassigned to schools. All-white and all-black schools were no longer permitted. "The time has come for the era of dual school systems to be ended," Thurgood wrote.

School desegregation was not the only major issue Thurgood dealt with during his twenty-four years as a Supreme Court justice. He took part in many other historical decisions.

Thurgood was a strong supporter of what are called First Amendment rights. These rights include the freedom to speak out and say what's on our minds; the freedom to print and distribute books, magazines, and papers; the freedom to worship as a person chooses; the freedom to assemble in meetings; and the right to petition the government when a group of people thinks something needs changing. In one Court decision dealing with a First Amendment issue, Thurgood wrote that "the right to receive information and ideas, regardless of their social worth, is fundamental to our free society." Then he added that if the First Amendment means anything, it means the government "has no business telling a man, sitting alone in his own house, what books he may read or what films he may watch. Our whole constitutional heritage rebels at the thought of giving government the power to control men's minds."

Thurgood's Supreme Court voting record, as well as the many decisions he wrote, had one thing in common. It reflected his great concern for the rights of those of our citizens who are poor and unfortunate. This concern led him to study records showing which people convicted of murder were most likely to be executed. He concluded it was poor people and minorities, especially African-Americans. For that reason, Thurgood came to believe that capital punishment—the death penalty—was the "ultimate form of discrimination." More than that, Thurgood Marshall believed capital punishment was "cruel and unusual." If that is so, capital punishment would be unconstitutional. The Eighth Amendment forbids cruel and unusual punishment.

Thurgood tried hard to convince his fellow justices that the Eighth Amendment did not permit a death penalty. He was not successful. But in one case in 1973, *Furman v. Georgia*, the Court did say that the way the death penalty had been used in the past was unjust. The justices agreed with Thurgood that some persons were more likely to be executed than others. As a result of the *Furman* decision, all state death penalties were "thrown out," and could no longer be used. If a state wanted the death penalty, it would have to rewrite its law to be more fair to minorities.

Some historians believe that history goes in cycles. Sometimes people want progress and change. At other times, people fear change and even yearn for things to go back to the way they used to be. As time went on, Thurgood became concerned that the same thing might happen to the civil rights gains of the 1950s and 1960s. Progress had been made back then. Now maybe people wanted to slow things down. Thurgood was concerned because of appointments being made to the Supreme Court. Republican presidents in the 1970s and 1980s appointed increasingly conservative justices. People with conservative ideas prefer to keep things the way they are, or even to go back to the way they were in former times. Conservatives tend to be cautious of change. Thurgood wanted to see a faster advance in personal freedom in many different areas. To express his frustration at how slowly the court sometimes moved, Thurgood wrote more than 1,800 *dissenting opinions,* or dissents. Dissents are essays that disagree with what the majority of justices say in their decision. The majority is those justices who voted with the winning side of a case. Of course, it is what the majority says that becomes the law of the land. But a dissent at least gives voice to other ideas on an issue.

Thurgood could often be gruff and fiery with those who did not see things his way. Yet he always kept his sense of humor. He liked to tell stories, and he loved to tell them with a funny twist. And he could joke freely with anyone, high or low. In the Supreme Court halls, he was known sometimes to greet the very proper Chief Justice Burger with a "What's shakin', chiefy baby?" He had a light touch with the plain fellows at his local barbershop, too. His job never "went to his head." He was, as he became known to many, "Mr. Civil Rights." He had started out as a young lawyer wanting to help change the world—and he did.

# Home at Last

When Thurgood wasn't deciding Supreme Court cases, he relaxed at home with his family. After living in Washington, D.C., for some time, he and Cissy bought a house in Falls Church, Virginia, and moved there with their two sons. Thurgood loved his family and spent most of his evenings at home, in spite of his demanding schedule. The family often watched TV together, and sometimes Thurgood played what he called "think games" with his boys. He hoped that they would one day go to college, then follow him into law. Thurgood, Jr., did, in fact, become a lawyer. John went into law enforcement. He became a Virginia State Trooper.

Thurgood kept up his love for Western movies all of his life. He was especially happy when the VCR was invented. Then he could play his favorites over and over again.

The Washington, D.C., area has a number of sports teams, both college and professional. Thurgood loyally followed the Baltimore Orioles baseball team—he loved baseball. And along with the rest of Washington, he cheered for the Redskins football team.

Thurgood liked all kinds of music. From his college days, he had a fondness for jazz. In his later years,

Thurgood preferred a more mellow sound. He listened to classical music while he relaxed. "I don't know all the titles and composers," he would tell his friends. "I just like it."

Thurgood suffered a heart attack in 1976. On his doctor's advice, he lightened his work schedule. He also tried to follow a healthier diet. That wasn't always easy. He loved to cook, and on weekends often sent Cissy out of the kitchen entirely. For the most part, Thurgood shrugged off the concern about his health and threw himself back into his work. When the press began suggesting that he was too sick and old to continue on the Court, Thurgood snapped back. So long as President Ronald Reagan was in the White House, he asserted, he would stay right where he was. The president, after all, had taken office at the advanced age of seventy. Furthermore, Thurgood believed that President Reagan had "done zero for civil rights." By staying on the Court, Thurgood hoped to remain in a position to keep the dream of equal rights alive.

Thurgood stayed on the Supreme Court until 1991. On June 27 of that year—five days before his eighty-third birthday—Thurgood announced that he was retiring. He was simply sick and tired, too weak to continue carrying a justice's heavy workload. He would at last step down and start taking it easy.

About a year later, on Independence Day, 1992, Thurgood Marshall visited Philadelphia's Independence Hall. Now lame and in a wheelchair, he was the guest of honor at the city's annual Fourth of July celebration.

Praise for the man and his career came from many

sources. A former law clerk said, "He dismantled the American apartheid." Apartheid is the kind of strict racial segregation once practiced in South Africa. And Senator Joseph Biden of Delaware commented that, "The Supreme Court has lost an historic justice—a hero for all America and for all times."

Thurgood was presented with the Liberty Medal. The medal is given to "an individual . . . from anywhere in the world that has demonstrated leadership and vision in the pursuit of liberty of conscience or freedom from oppression, ignorance, and deprivation." Only three other people have received this high honor. They are Lech Walesa, the Polish union leader who helped bring democracy to his country and later became its president; former U.S. president Jimmy Carter, who dedicated his retirement years to promoting human rights and free elections around the world; and Oscar Arias Sanchez, the former Costa Rican president who led the efforts to bring peace to Central America.

Thurgood Marshall died of heart failure on January 24, 1993. News of his death made every newspaper and TV news program in the nation—and many in the world. The stories outlined his career, emphasizing his twenty-four-year service on the Supreme Court. But everyone agreed on what was his most famous accomplishment, the one that had the most effect on how people live day-to-day. It was his part in the *Brown v. Board of Education* case. Thurgood Marshall was the lawyer who "devised the legal strategy that ended school desegregation."

William and Norma Marshall would have been

proud of their second son. Through all of his life, his mother's values had been buried deep in Thurgood's memory, along with his father's respect for words. There was also the Constitution that the teenage Thurgood was made to memorize. He might have resented it at the time, but he drew upon that document for the rest of his life. Finally, there was both the fair and the unjust treatment he had received at the hands of whites. He learned there were good and bad people in every group. The experiences of his life combined to shape a lawyer, a good one. One who dedicated his great talents to the pursuit of justice. And in helping free his own community in America, he assured greater freedom for all Americans.

Thurgood Marshall left a stunning legacy. More than any other single person in the last half of the twentieth century, Thurgood Marshall demanded that the judicial branch of our government live up to the promise that "all men are created equal." It was his court victory over separate schools that sparked the civil rights movement. Two civil rights acts and a voter rights act became law in the 1960s. One civil rights act made it possible for people to buy or rent any house they could afford. Another made such practices as separate lunch counters and drinking fountains illegal. The voter rights act guaranteed the right to vote to adults regardless of race. It is remarkable that one man was responsible for so much change. Thurgood Marshall was one of those people in our history who made a difference. Because of

Thurgood Marshall, America is closer today to the ideal of equal justice for all.

Summing up his life and his contributions, Thurgood said of himself on the day he retired: "I guess you could say, 'He did what he could with what he had.'"

# GLOSSARY

**affidavit** – a statement by a witness, revealing what the person saw.

**appeal** – to request that a higher court listen to a case.

**boycott** – the refusal to buy a particular product or to shop in certain stores.

**brief** – a detailed essay written by lawyers about cases they are appealing to higher courts.

**civil rights** – rights found in the United States Constitution that are guaranteed to all Americans.

**Civil War** – a war fought from 1861-1865 in the United States between the northern and southern states.

**closing statements** – speeches made at the end of a trial by both the attorney for the plaintiff and the attorney for the defense.

**Constitution** – the U.S. Constitution is a document that states the role of the national government.

**defendant** – in a court case, the side that is said to have hurt the plaintiff in some way.

**Democratic party** – the oldest of America's two main political parties.

**depression** – a slowing down of a nation's economy, when jobs are hard to find and people are losing the jobs they already have.

**discrimination** – the act of treating one group of people differently from other groups.

**dissenting opinion** – an essay written by one of the justices of the Supreme Court that states feelings and ideas that differ from the majority.

**Emancipation Proclamation** – a document written by President Abraham Lincoln that freed most of the slaves in the United States. The Thirteenth Amendment freed the rest.

**general election** – an election held in November in the United States that determines which candidates will win government offices.

**Jim Crow laws** – a slang term for the segregation laws passed by Southern governments in the years following the Civil War. *Jim Crow laws* made it difficult and illegal for whites and African-Americans to associate with one another.

**Ku Klux Klan** – the KKK was founded in 1869 by former Confederate soldiers in Tennessee and eventually had members all across the United States. The group sought to keep African-Americans from voting or holding political office. The Klan was brutal in its use of violence against African-Americans.

**lawsuit** – a case brought before a court by a person who feels he or she has been wronged in some way.

**majority opinion** – an essay written by a member of the court on the winning side of a case. The essay explains what the court decided and why it decided as such.

**NAACP** – the National Association for the Advancement of Colored People was founded in 1909 for the purpose of achieving equal rights for African-Americans and eliminating discrimination based upon skin color or race.

**oral arguments** – speeches given by lawyers before a court of law.

**plaintiff** – a person who goes to court with a lawsuit against someone.

**poll tax** – a tax that had to be paid in many Southern states in the past in order for people to vote.

**precedent** – the first court decision on a particular subject. Precedents are referred to by lawyers and judges in future cases of similar situations.

**primary election** – an election in which voters choose who the official Democratic and Republican candidates will be in the next general election.

**Republican party** – one of America's two main political parties.

**segregation** – the separation of people on the basis of skin color.

**third degree** – torture, including beatings and scare tactics, used by police officers to get a suspect to admit he or she committed a crime.

**unconstitutional** – a term applied to a law or activity that cannot be allowed because it is against the rights guaranteed by the U.S. Constitution.

**Union** – the Northern side during the Civil War.

**U.S. Court of Appeals** – eleven courts, sometimes called circuit courts, that make up the middle level of the federal court system in the United States.

**U.S. District Court** – the lowest of the federal courts in the United States.

**U.S. Supreme Court** – the highest, or most powerful, court in the United States.

**white supremacy** – the idea that white people should hold all political offices and make all the decisions regarding the citizens of a country.

*Highlights in the Life of*
# THURGOOD MARSHALL

**1908** Thoroughgood (Thurgood) Marshall is born on July 2 in Baltimore, Maryland. Theodore Roosevelt is president of the United States.

**1909** The Marshall family moves to Harlem.

**1914** The Marshall family returns to Baltimore.

**1915** In the second grade, *Thoroughgood* Marshall changes his name to *Thurgood* Marshall.

**1922** Thurgood Marshall is arrested for hitting a white man.

**1925** At sixteen, Thurgood Marshall graduates from Frederick Douglass High School. At seventeen, Marshall begins his freshman year at Lincoln University in Chester, Pennsylvania.

**1929** Thurgood Marshall and Vivian "Buster" Burey are married on September 4. The Great Depression begins when the New York Stock Exchange crashes on October 29.

**1930** Thurgood Marshall applies to the University of Maryland Law School. He is turned down because of his race. Marshall enrolls at Howard University.

**1933** Thurgood Marshall graduates first in his class. He opens a private law office in Baltimore.

**1935**  Thurgood Marshall files suit to desegregate the University of Maryland Law School.  On June 18, he argues the law school case, *Murray v. University of Maryland*.  Marshall wins.  The judge orders the law school desegregated on June 25.

**1936**  Thurgood Marshall is appointed the NAACP's assistant special counsel in New York City.

**1941**  Thurgood Marshall travels to Oklahoma to defend W.D. Lyons against murder charges.

**1944**  Thurgood Marshall argues successfully in *Smith v. Allwright*, and the Supreme Court confirms the right of thousands of Southern blacks to vote.

**1946**  The NAACP awards Thurgood Marshall the Spingarn Medal, its highest honor.

**1954**  In *Brown v. Board of Education*, the Supreme Court accepts Thurgood Marshall's argument against the separation of children into white and black schools.  America's public schools are ordered to desegregate.

**1955**  Buster, Thurgood Marshall's wife of twenty-five years, dies.  Later that year, he marries Cecilia "Cissy" Suyat.

**1956**  Thurgood Marshall argues his case successfully, and the Supreme Court declares the Montgomery, Alabama, bus segregation law unconstitutional.

**1961**   John F. Kennedy is inaugurated on January 20. Thurgood Marshall travels to London to help write the constitution for the newly independent African nation, Kenya. President Kennedy sends Thurgood Marshall to Sierra Leone as the American representative to that country's independence ceremonies. JFK appoints Thurgood Marshall to the U.S. Court of Appeals for the Second Circuit, serving New York, Connecticut, and Vermont.

**1963**   President Kennedy is assassinated on November 22. Vice President Lyndon Johnson becomes president.

**1965**   Thurgood Marshall is appointed U.S. Solicitor General by President Johnson.

**1967**   President Johnson appoints Thurgood Marshall to the U.S. Supreme Court.

**1991**   Nearly eighty-three years old, Thurgood Marshall announces his retirement from the Supreme Court.

**1993**   Thurgood Marshall dies on January 24.

# For Further Study

## More Books to Read

*Freedom Bound: A History of America's Civil Rights Movement.* Robert Weisbrot (Norton)

*Stride Toward Freedom.* Reverend Martin Luther King, Jr. (HarperRow)

*They Had A Dream: The Civil Rights Struggle from Frederick Douglass to Marcus Garvey to Martin Luther King, Jr.* Jules Archer (Viking)

*Thurgood Marshall.* Lisa Aldred (Chelsea House)

*Thurgood Marshall: The Fight for Equal Justice.* Debra Hess (Silver Burdett)

*Thurgood Marshall: First African-American Supreme Court Justice.* Carol Greene (Childrens Press)

## Videos

*Black America: The Civil Rights Movement.* (Centre Communications)

*The Civil Rights Movement.* (RMI Media Productions)

*Eyes on the Prize.* (PBS Video)

*The March on Washington Remembered.* (Encyclopedia Britannica Educational Corporation)

*Supreme Court.* (American Bar Association)

*Thurgood Marshall.* (Schlessinger Video Productions)

*Thurgood Marshall: Portrait of an American Hero.* (PBS Video)

*We Shall Overcome.* (California Newsreel)

# Index

Baltimore (Maryland) 4, 5, 6, 10, 11, 15, 17, 29, 32, 35, 36, 37, 38, 42, 52, 53
boycotts 37, 38, 80-85
Briggs family 68, 69, 70, 74
*Briggs v. Elliott* 72, 73
*Brown v. Board of Education* 54, 73, 74, 78, 90, 97
bus boycott (Montgomery, Alabama) 80, 82, 83, 84, 85

civil rights 24, 37, 38, 40, 42, 47, 53, 69, 72, 79, 80, 83, 84, 85, 86, 87, 93, 94, 96, 98
Clark, Kenneth 71, 72
Constitution, U.S. 18, 19, 20, 23, 28, 35, 60, 63, 85, 98
Court of Appeals, U.S. 55, 64, 86, 87, 89

"doll study" 71

Eighth Amendment 92, 93
Emancipation Proclamation 63

First Amendment 91, 92

*Furman v. Georgia* 92, 93

Gandhi, Mahatma 84

Houston, Charles 32, 34, 38, 40, 41, 42, 43
Howard University 31, 32, 33, 72

Jim Crow laws 4, 32, 41, 42, 47, 63, 82, 91
Johnson, President Lyndon B. 56, 88, 89

Kennedy, President John F. 55, 85, 86, 87
Kenya 86
King, Dr. Martin Luther, Jr. 83, 84, 85
Ku Klux Klan 11, 46, 47, 50, 61, 64, 90

Lincoln, President Abraham 63
Looby, Alexander 48, 49
Lyons, W. D. 43, 44, 45, 46

Marshall, Cecilia ("Cissy") (wife) 56, 57, 79, 80, 87, 88, 89, 90, 95, 96

107